PRAISE FOR THE CATHOLIC TABLE

"The Catholic Table *serves up a banquet of good sense infused
with theology, blending practical advice with startling insights into
our relationship with food—and on the side, what else but recipes?
This is Emily Stimpson Chapman at her witty, well-educated,
accessible best.*"

—SIMCHA FISHER, AUTHOR OF
THE SINNER'S GUIDE TO NATURAL FAMILY PLANNING

"*As an admitted non-foodie, I was surprised and delighted by
Emily Stimpson Chapman's* The Catholic Table. *Chock-full of
practical and poignant thoughts and ideas, this book is mentally,
spiritually and physically nutritious.*"

—LISA M. HENDEY, FOUNDER OF CATHOLICMOM.COM
AND AUTHOR OF *THE GRACE OF YES*

"*If you've ever struggled with eating too much or too little, binging
or purging, obsessively counting calories or panicking over every
food label in the store, Emily Stimpson Chapman is your guide to
a better relationship with food. After reading* The Catholic Table,
*you'll not only be convinced that how you approach food is a vital
part of living out your Christian faith, you'll wish you could land
yourself on Chapman's next dinner guest list.*"

—ZOE ROMANOWSKY,
FREELANCE WRITER, BLOGGER, AND CONSULTANT

"The Catholic Table *is a beautiful elaboration of Emily Stimpson Chapman's blog by the same name. It looks at the foodie landscape and contrasts it with a Catholic theology of food. The Church's wisdom, quotes from Saints, stories of food miracles, the author's past struggles with eating, and even recipes show us how a proper respect for food leads to peace and joy. I will never look at my sandwiches in the same way!"*

—PATTI MAGUIRE ARMSTRONG,
CATHOLIC AUTHOR AND JOURNALIST

"The Catholic Table *is an inspiring tutorial on finding strength through faith and practical solutions when dealing with serious eating issues. Readers will feel like they're walking alongside the author as they deal with the challenges of eating disorders. They will find solace and healing, both physical and spiritual, in real time."*

—RITA NADER HEIKENFELD,
EDITOR OF ABOUTEATING.COM

THE CATHOLIC TABLE

Finding Joy Where Food and Faith Meet

THE CATHOLIC TABLE

Finding Joy Where Food and Faith Meet

EMILY STIMPSON CHAPMAN

EMMAUS ROAD PUBLISHING

Steubenville, Ohio
www.emmausroad.org

Emmaus Road Publishing
1468 Parkview Circle
Steubenville, Ohio 43952

Library of Congress Control Number: 2016954678
ISBN: 978-1-941447-99-4

Cover design and layout by Margaret Ryland

Image © Vicki Grafton Photography, courtesy of Stocksy.

To my husband, Christopher.
There's no one else for whom I'd rather spend
a lifetime cooking.

"Had Aristotle cooked, he would have written a good deal more."

SOR JUANA INÉS DE LA CRUZ

TABLE OF CONTENTS

ACKNOWLEDGMENTS

If I ever write a book about wedding planning, it will include a pointed piece of advice for writers: Don't attempt to write a book and plan a wedding at the same time. Both are happy things in themselves, but the combination of the two does not make for a happy author or a happy bride.

Fortunately for me, I had the most patient of publishers and fiancées. So, much thanks is owed to all the people at Emmaus Road Publishing—especially Scott Hahn, Rob Corzine, Andrew Jones, and Melissa Knaggs—for their willingness to work with me and wait a little bit longer than expected for *The Catholic Table*.

Even more thanks is owed to my husband, Christopher, who became a world-class expert in talking me off ledges during the months it took to write this book and plan the day that marked the first in our new life together. For his love, his encouragement, and his advice on the book throughout, he has more than earned a lifetime of well-cooked meals.

Some of the chapters in this book began as blog posts at *The Catholic Table*. Others began as essays for *Lay Witness*, Our Sunday Visitor newspaper, and CatholicVote. I'm grateful for the opportunities those outlets have given me through the years to ruminate on food and more fully develop my thoughts on the subject.

I'd also like to thank Sr. Timothy Prokes, FSE, one of the wisest scholars and holiest women I have ever known. Years ago, when I was first starting to articulate my Eucharistic understanding of food, her encouragement and guidance were a profound help. Not only did her thinking on the subject shape my own thinking, but her support of my work gave me confidence to move forward. She is an amazing writer and beautiful Bride of Christ, and anyone who reads her or knows her is better off for it.

And of course, thanks as always to my trusted team of heavenly intercessors: the Blessed Virgin, St. Joseph, St. Catherine of Siena, St. Edith Stein, St. Gianna Beretta Molla, and St. John Paul II. Please keep the praying up, so that someday, I can join you all at the dinner party to beat all dinner parties.

Kitchen Poems

About a century ago, the ever-wise G. K. Chesterton observed, "Poets have been mysteriously silent on the subject of cheese."

Truth.

Sure, the bards have penned countless phrases about love and loss. They've waxed rhapsodic about fair-skinned maidens and dark-haired ladies. There is no end to the couplets they've coined about God and man, life and death, war and peace.

But a sonnet about a really good Stilton? Nada. A ballad to a first-rate triple-crème Brie? The silence is deafening.

Frankly, the only problem I have with Chesterton's otherwise perfectly sage observation is that it didn't go far enough. It's not just the subject of cheese upon which the poets' pens have run dry. It's also cheesecake. And espresso. And a really big bowl of garlic-roasted Brussels sprouts.

There's so much to say about garlic-roasted Brussels sprouts.

I'd blame this glaring shortcoming in the world of poetry on the dominance of male poets, but Elizabeth Barrett Browning and Sylvia Plath didn't get the job done either. Not enough time in the kitchen, I suppose.

If more peasant women had the time to write verse, the history of poetry might be different. Alas, it is not. And, with an even bigger alas, I confess that the book you have in your hands will not correct the problem anytime soon.

Apologies, but I'm not a poet, just an overworked Catholic writer who convinced her publisher to let her write a book about food—the meaning of it, the cooking of it, the serving of it, the eating of it, the sacramentality of it, and, most important, the glory of it.

My hope, however, (in fact, my prayer) is that this little volume inspires some aspiring bard to do what I can't and get cracking on that cheese poetry. The world is waiting. I am waiting.

In the meantime, room still exists for some decent, solid prose on the subject of food. So, that's what I aim to give you.

WONDERS AND WONDER

Some of what follows will sound familiar to those of you who've read my various essays on all things food related, published in the Catholic press and on my own blog (also called *The Catholic Table*) over the last decade.

I've written so much about what we eat because, unlike the poets, I am of the mind that there is nothing ordinary about food. By God's grace, the simplest bowl of soup and the humblest hunk of cheese have the power to become an occasion of grace, drawing friends and family together around a shared table to build a shared life.

Even more remarkably, by God's even greater grace, the plainest piece of bread and the cheapest cup of wine can actually become grace. In the Eucharist, they become the Body, Blood, Soul, and Divinity of Jesus Christ, imparting the life of God to our wounded, weary, totally undeserving selves.

That's the twofold gift of food. On the natural level, it can work wonders—comforting us, healing us, nurturing us. On the supernatural level, food becomes Wonder—God hidden in a piece of bread.

American Catholics tend to focus on the latter gift. We believe in the supernatural truth about food. We proclaim it every time we attend Mass. If we go online and some unsuspecting Protestant says otherwise, we make fast to correct their flawed theology with a dozen different proofs.

In our own lives, however, many of us struggle to understand and receive food as a natural gift. In how we eat, how we cook, how we think about food and our bodies, we struggle to appreciate food the way God meant us to appreciate it. Some of us eat too much food. Or we eat too little. Often, we eat without gratitude, without charity, without respect. Some fear food. Others idolize it. Occasionally, we confuse health with virtue. More than occasionally, we turn food into a tool, a way to deal with hurt, confusion, fear, anxiety, shame, guilt, passion, insecurity, and a dozen other problems for which food bears none of the blame.

Since Eden, men and women have roundly abused the good gifts God entrusted to us. Food is no exception.

It doesn't have to be that way, though.

FAMINE TO FEAST

The Church, in her great wisdom, offers us a way to see the world that can restore the gift of food to its proper place. In her teachings on grace, the Eucharist, the virtues, fasting, hospitality, and the body, she charts a course for us quite different from the one the world urges us to follow. Fortunately for us, her course leads not only to peace, joy, and community, but also to some really good dinners. This book is my attempt to sum up that course and help you follow it.

As you'll discover (if you're the sort of person who reads the footnotes), *The Catholic Table* draws on the thinking and writing of people much more clever than I: St. John Paul II, Leon Kass, Robert Farrar Capon, Sr. Timothy Prokes, Caroline Bynum Walker, and others.

It also draws on my own experience of eating at the Catholic table. I first sat down at the table sixteen years ago, after six long years in the wasteland of anorexia and binge eating. I'll talk more about my journey out of that wasteland throughout this book. For now, it suffices to say that living for so long in that place of famine and fear made me appreciate all the more the blessed place that the Catholic table is.

Again, the peace. And the cheese.

The cheese is really good at the Catholic table.

If you're already tempted to try your hand at an Ode to Humboldt Fog, feel free to toddle off right now. This book isn't going anywhere, and time's a wasting.

If, however, you want to get a better handle on just how disordered the American culture's attitude towards food is, read on.

CHAPTER ONE

Unclean

Surveying America's Food Landscape

<p style="text-align:justify">

Before I write anything else, I have a confession to make: Every once in a while—for example, when pictures of decapitated Christians in the Middle East flash across my MacBook screen—I wonder if I should continue spending my days writing a book about food. Urgent problems and grievous tragedies abound in this world, and cheese just doesn't seem that important when compared to religious genocide.

Then, I remember the passage from C. S. Lewis' *Mere Christianity* where he attempts to demonstrate to his readers that pornography stems from an unhealthy—not healthy—attitude towards sex:

> You can get a large audience together for a strip-tease act—that is, to watch a girl undress on the stage. Now suppose you came to a country where you could fill a theatre by simply bringing a covered plate on to the stage and then slowly lifting the cover so as to let everyone see, just before the lights went out, that it contained a mutton chop

or a bit of bacon. Would you not think that in that country something had gone wrong with the appetite for food?

With that reminder, I get back to work.

FETISHIZING FOOD

The first time I read Lewis' words, I was a sophomore in college. It was 1995, and I agreed with him wholeheartedly. The idea of people gathering together for the sole purpose of ogling food seemed ridiculous. I mean, how messed up could you be to get all hot and bothered about a piece of bacon?

Twenty years later, when I posted a photo of bacon on my food blog and described it as "sultry," Lewis' words flashed through my mind. And I cringed.

These days, Lewis' metaphor makes less sense because unnatural excitement over a piece of bacon is practically an everyday occurrence online. Food blogs' bread and butter are perfectly lit photos of alluring vegetables, glistening with oil, while Pinterest is little more than a virtual peep show for baked goods. The common term for these artfully arranged close-ups of plated delicacies is "food porn." Vulgar. But accurate.

Many of the people looking at the pictures of food that now populate the digital landscape will never try to make the recipes accompanying those pictures. Some of the people doing the looking wouldn't even eat the food if someone else cooked it for them. Often that's the very reason they're looking. Because they "can't" have the food in the picture; it contains too much fat or too much dairy or too much gluten. "Virtual eating" is their poor man's substitute for the real thing.[1]

_____

[1] Ron Rosenbaum, "Anthony Bourdain's Theory on the Foodie Revolution," *Smithsonian Magazine*, July 2014, http://www.smithsonianmag.com/arts-culture/anthony-bourdains-theory-foodie-revolution-180951848/; Molly

That's not to say cooking magazines or food blogs are problematic in themselves. Many a food blog has come to my rescue when I'm planning my weekly menu or throwing a dinner party. I like food blogs. Heck, I run a food blog. Food blogs aren't the problem.

Rather, the problem is the rise of virtual eating—what food writer Ron Rosenbaum calls the "fetishization of food"—gazing upon food for the sheer pleasure of gazing on it, with no intention of cooking or eating something similar. Such gazing is . . . well . . . odd.[2]

It also is a sign of our culture's disordered attitude about food. And it's not the only sign.

"Eat without scruple whatever God has prepared for you at the common table . . . whatever God provides for you, take that with simplicity of heart from his hand."

St. Philip Neri

DISORDERED

Summing up the silliness in America's food culture is no small task. There's just so much of it. I'll give it the old college try, though.

To start with, while whole groups of people might be ogling food together online, when it comes to the actual eating of food, as often as not, we eat alone.

Gone are the days when people (almost) always and (almost) everywhere took food at a table, with others. These days, the world is our table. We eat breakfast in our cars, lunch at our desks, dinner

---

O'Neil, "Food Porn," Alternet, October 23, 2003, http://www.alternet.org/story/17037/food_porn.

[2] Rosenbaum, 2014.

on our sofas, and snacks as we walk through our city's streets. Fifty-eight percent of Americans routinely eat alone. Only 41 percent of U.S. families regularly sit down together anymore, at a table, television off, silverware in hand. Whole swaths of American kids don't even know the meaning of "the family dinner" anymore. [3]

Perhaps the lack of talking over meals and sharing those meals with others contributes to another sign of America's food problem: our ever-expanding waistlines. In 2012, Americans spent more than sixty billion dollars—ten zeros six times over—trying to shed unwanted pounds. Despite that, more than two out of three adults in this country are overweight. One in three is obese. [4]

Those who aren't overweight are often underweight. Anywhere from five to eight percent of American women struggle with anorexia or bulimia; they either eat too little or purge what they do eat as soon as possible. That's an estimated six to ten million women. Millions more struggle with "pathological dieting" or subclinical eating disorders. [5]

Then, there are those who fit into the newest category of disordered eating: orthorexia nervosa, which entails having an unhealthy obsession with healthy eating. People struggling with orthorexia fear additives and preservatives, hormones in their meat, antibiotics in their chickens, pesticides on their greens, and gluten in their cookies almost as much as anorexics fear fat on their plate. More than just a desire to eat healthy, orthorexia is a compulsion to

---

[3]   CBS News, "How Americans Eat Today," January 12, 2010, http://www.cbsnews.com/2100-500165_162-6086647.html.

[4]   Geoff Williams, "The Heavy Price of Losing Weight," *U.S. News and World Report*, January 2, 2013, http://money.usnews.com/money/personal-finance/articles/2013/01/02/the-heavy-price-of-losing-weight; Douglas Main, "Seven in 10 American Adults Are Overweight or Obese," *Newsweek*, June 22, 2015, http://www.newsweek.com/7-10-american-adults-are-overweight-or-obese-345723.

[5]   See data collected from multiple surveys, compiled at Eating Disorder Hope: http://www.eatingdisorderhope.com/information/statistics-studies.

"eat right" and "be good." There is no occasional piece of Domino's pizza or Little Debbie snack cake for orthorexics. Or, if there is, overwhelming guilt, not enjoyment, follows.[6]

PATRON SAINTS OF COOKING

ANTHONY OF EGYPT

God has a gift for irony. That's the only way to explain how a fourth-century ascetic, who lived on little more than the occasional scrap of bread, wound up as the patron saint of butchers.

Born into wealth in 251, St. Anthony eventually gave away his fortune and fled civilization to live a life of solitude and penance. Unfortunately for him, his penance became, in part, the crowds of admirers who followed him into the desert. Many came to hear him teach. Others came for healing. It's believed that the future saint was particularly skilled in healing diseases of the skin using a special concoction made of pig fat.

After his death, those who knew of his expertise with medicinal pig fat often depicted Anthony with a pig or two. Eventually, that led those who worked with pigs in other capacities (namely butchering them) to claim Anthony as their own particular intercessor. Hopefully, the saint, who lived as a strict vegan during his lifetime, doesn't mind.

It's easy to dismiss eating disorders as uncommon or rare. But orthorexics, anorexics, and bulimics simply sit at the extreme end of an increasingly common trend: defining virtue in terms of the food we eat.

---

[6] Karin Kratina, "Orthorexia Nervosa," National Eating Disorders Association, https://www.nationaleatingdisorders.org/orthorexia-nervosa.

Spend a week listening to how people talk about what they had for dinner, and chances are you'll hear the words "good" and "bad" applied not so much to the food eaten, but rather to the person doing the eating. We're good when we eat a salad. We're bad when we eat cheesecake.

Whether it's calories people care about or the absence of preservatives, for many, eating now comes with a moral weight. You can sleep with whomever you want, whenever you want, but fail to buy hormone-free milk and you best prepare yourself for some good old-fashioned judgment.

Case in point? The comments I recently stumbled across on one of my favorite food blogs, *Budget Bytes*, while doing a little menu planning.

"It would be so worth the extra money not to be eating a poisonous product," sneered one commenter, when the blog host failed to specify *organic* frozen corn in one of her recipes. "I'll be making an organic version because I care about how my food is grown!"

"Coconut oil would be more virtuous than vegetable oil," pontificated another commenter on the same recipe.

Note: "More virtuous." Not "healthier." Not "tastier." Not even "better." More virtuous.

"It is not food that is evil but gluttony, not the begetting of children but unchastity, not material things but avarice, not esteem but self-esteem. This being so, it is only the misuse of things that is evil, and such misuse occurs when the intellect fails to cultivate its natural powers."

ST. MAXIMUS THE CONFESSOR

DISTORTED

Our culture-wide struggle with food isn't just about what we eat. It's also about how we're expected to look despite what we eat.

While the average American has grown heavier by the year, the ideal presented to us on television screens and in the pages of fashion magazines has grown ever thinner. Today's average model typically weighs 25 percent below what experts consider a healthy bodyweight. A model who wears a size six is considered "plus size."[7]

Cultures have always had their own standards of beauty, and most people have fallen short of those standards. But in days gone by, most people weren't treated to a steady diet of images featuring the most beautiful of the beautiful. Thanks to the mass media, we now are. It's not surprising, therefore, in a culture more concerned with the material than the spiritual, that four out of five women, including those at a healthy weight, claim serious dissatisfaction with their bodies.

What is surprising, but maybe shouldn't be, is how deep that dissatisfaction goes.

Over the past decade, numerous studies on body image have turned up results that show large swaths of America's female population veering headlong into crazy territory. For example . . .

Two out of five women say they'd trade five years of their lives to reach their "ideal" weight.

Adolescent girls say they're more afraid of becoming fat than nuclear war, cancer, or losing their parents.

Twenty-three percent of American women ages 18–34 would rather lose their ability to read than lose their figures.

And a full half would opt to get hit by a bus rather than get fat.[8]

[7] Edward Lovett, "Most Models Meet Criteria for Anorexia," ABC News, January 12, 2012, http://abcnews.go.com/blogs/headlines/2012/01/most-models-meet-criteria-for-anorexia-size-6-is-plus-size-magazine.

[8] The Council on Size and Weight Discrimination, Facts and Figures, accessed

All that is to say that tens of millions of women consider being thin more important than being smart, virtuous, or *alive*. Their identity, their self-worth is wrapped up in a clothing size and a number on a scale. Millions of those women (and more than a few men) are starving themselves to get the number they want. Millions more are disassociated from their bodies, food, and the human community, unable to do the basic things men and women managed to do for many a long millennia—properly feed and care for themselves.

Food porn is the least of our problems.

Clean Eating

In the 1990s, Snackwell's made a mint off of America's obsession with fat-free eating. Today, however, profits lie elsewhere: in the current craze over eating "clean." Depending on who you talk to, "clean eating" might mean avoiding artificial colors, flavors, and preservatives; or it might mean eating nothing that isn't organically grown, sustainably harvested, grass-fed, and free-ranged. Either way, the organic food business has become one of the food industry's biggest moneymakers, grossing $42 billion in 2014.[9]

There's much to be said for "clean eating." In general, snacking on food made from ingredients you can't pronounce and pumped full of hormones is a bad idea. At the same time, modern farming methods and genetic crop modifications prevent millions of people from starving to death each year. That's kind of a big deal, too.

May 20, 2016, http://www.cswd.org/docs/facts.html.

[9]   "U.S. Organic Food Industry: Statistics and Facts," *Statista,* accessed on May 20, 2016, http://www.statista.com/topics/1047/organic-food-industry.

The scientific community is divided on the clean eating question. Some researchers see advantages to going organic. Others disagree, pointing to the potential dangers of organic pesticides and potential benefits of genetically modified (GMO) crops. The Church, being the Church and not the U.S. Food and Drug Administration, has no opinion on the question. So, if it makes you feel better to keep your family's diet as natural as possible, and you can do that while still being generous to the poor, go for it. On the other hand, if you're more concerned about simply getting food on the table than making sure that food is certified organic, you're not failing as a parent or a person.

If, however, you make everyone around you miserable in your quest to eat clean—tormenting unsuspecting waiters with soliloquys on the evils of vegetable oil and chastising your mother-in-law for serving your kids pre-washed, pre-cut baby carrots—that is a problem. We're all going to die someday, clean eating or not. When that day comes, it will matter more if we were kind to others and received what was prepared for us with gratitude than if we won the Clean Eating Award.

That's because when we get to the pearly gates what really needs to be clean is our soul, not our diet.

ALIENATION

Which brings us back to why—despite starving children in Korea, bloodthirsty caliphs in the Middle East, and transgendered men in women's restrooms—food merits more than a moment of our attention.

The physical consequences of our disordered attitudes toward food are clear enough. Whether a person is overweight or underweight, exercising too little or too much, they put stress on their heart and other vital organs, damaging muscles and bones alike. That's bad. It's bad for individuals, it's bad for families, and it's bad for the American taxpayer. Recent studies estimate that growing rates of obesity accounted for at least 27 percent of health care inflation between 1987 and 2001. By 2018, it's expected to account for 21 percent of the country's overall health care spending.[10]

But rising health care costs are hardly the greatest problem wrought by our culture's disordered relationship with food. That honor goes to the spiritual damage that occurs when we don't see food rightly and live in accord with what we see.

The guilt about eating too much or too little; the shame about binging and purging; the hatred of our bodies because they don't conform to cultural expectations; the alienation from others created either by circumstance or our own self-imposed food choices; the time spent obsessing over food, what we will eat or won't eat; the constant dwelling on self and the neglect of others; the failure to love, nurture, and nourish those around us because we're too preoccupied with what goes into our belly; the handing on of bad habits and bad attitudes about food to our children; the breakdown of community as people become too busy to eat with one another; and ultimately, the separation from God that comes from turning in on ourselves—that's where our culture's problem with food can lead.

That's where it is leading.

It's easy to dismiss disordered attitudes towards food as a "First World Problem." But the devil doesn't. He is an opportunist who

---

[10] Ceci Connolly, "Obesity Gets Part of Blame for Health Care Costs," *The Washington Post*, October 20, 2004, http://www.washingtonpost.com/wp-dyn/articles/A46123-2004Oct19.html; Pierre L. Yong, Robert S Saunders, and LeighAnne Olsen, eds., "Introduction," *The Healthcare Imperative: Lowering Costs and Improving Outcomes* (Washington, DC: National Academies Press, 2010), 3.

knows how to make the most of the tools at his disposal. Give him a half-crazed, power hungry dictator, and he'll see how much wrath and despair he can engender with a nice famine or enforced terror policy. Give him a society flush with wealth and food, and he'll do what he can to evoke some good old-fashioned vanity and gluttony via CrossFit and Jenny Craig.

That's why learning to see food with Catholic eyes is so important; it robs the devil of one of his favorite weapons against twenty-first-century Americans.

Food isn't just about calories and fat, vitamins and minerals, additives and preservatives. It's about God. It's about community. It's about life. Food is one of God's most precious gifts, a sign of the Lord's goodness, abundance, creativity, and love. Most important, it's the very thing that God becomes for us in the Eucharist.

For those reasons and more, food matters. And when we see food for what it really is, life changes. Families change. Communities change. We change.

I know because a Catholic understanding of food changed me.

Grandma Miller's Pumpkin Bread

Growing up, it wasn't Thanksgiving or Christmas without my Grandma Miller's pumpkin bread. It still isn't.

Ingredients

3 ½ cups flour

3 cups sugar

½ teaspoon baking powder

1 teaspoon baking soda

1½ teaspoon salt

1 teaspoon cloves

1 teaspoon cinnamon

1 teaspoon nutmeg

2 cups pumpkin puree

1 cup vegetable oil

1 cup water

4 eggs

2 cups walnuts, chopped

Preheat oven to 325°. Mix dry ingredients together; set aside. Mix eggs, sugar, oil, water, and pumpkin together. Add dry ingredients to wet ingredients. Fold in nuts. Divide into two greased pans and bake for 90 minutes or until toothpick comes out clean.

CHAPTER TWO

Wasteland
My Hungry Years

O n a frosty Saturday night in January of 2016, I stood where I stand on most Saturday nights: at my stove, in my kitchen, cooking dinner. That Saturday was special, though. The night before, my boyfriend (now husband) Christopher asked me to marry him. I said yes before he had time to take a breath.

Our engagement was a long time coming. Nine years of friendship, thirteen months of dating, and a host of complications figured into our history. His decision to propose and my decision to accept was an occasion for much celebrating. And around here, we're quite good at celebrating.

The festivities began around 6:00 p.m., but Chris arrived early. He took care of a few chores around the house while I started chopping. Risotto was on the menu for the night—a Caprese risotto with tomatoes, basil, and fresh mozzarella. The kitchen smelled like summer.

I was still chopping onions when my friend Tom arrived, a bottle of wine, two kinds of olives, and three kinds of cheese in hand. After that, my friend Dave appeared at the backdoor. With him he brought a slab of pork belly that he'd recently cured into bacon. Dave is a gift from God.

As other friends arrived, we stood in the kitchen: me at the stove, patiently stirring the risotto; everyone else around the kitchen table, sampling the cheeses, meats, and olives; all of us sipping on the first bottle of wine we opened—a Montepulciano from Italy.

By the time the risotto reached a rich, creamy state of perfection, we'd finished one bottle of wine and moved on to the second—a Cabernet Franc from Washington's wine country.

That bottle, along with an extraordinary Bordeaux, came with us to the table. We bowed our heads, gave thanks to God for the food before us, then feasted on the risotto, served up with garlic roasted Brussels sprouts and some crusty bread.

For the next two hours we sat at the table—candles lit—talking, laughing, telling stories.

At the end of the night, I did the dishes, kissed my new fiancée goodbye, and happily went to bed. There was no guilt about the amount of bacon and cheese I'd eaten. There was no anxiety about the number of glasses of wine I'd consumed. I was satisfied, but not full; merry, but not drunk.

The dinner party, like so many other dinner parties that I've hosted, was a graced one, giving me no cause for self-recrimination. I'd eaten with gratitude and joy, exercising just the right amount of temperance and taking my ultimate satisfaction not so much in the food cooked, but in the community my cooking helped create.

In short, my dinner party was everything a dinner party should be. It was also everything I'd once thought impossible.

---

*"In general, give the body rather too much food than
too little."*

St. Philip Neri

HUNGER

Twenty-two years ago, when I was nineteen, I stopped eating. Not completely, just mostly. I ate enough to stay alive, to keep my grades up, and to keep my parents from pulling me out of school. No more.

Eight months earlier, I had begun college maybe ten pounds overweight. By April of my freshman year, thanks to too much pizza and not enough exercise, that number ballooned to twenty. I knew I needed to lose those extra pounds. I wasn't strong. I wasn't fit. I wasn't healthy. My body made me uncomfortable, and I felt ashamed of it. But I was so focused on keeping the grades my scholarship demanded of me that dieting was never more than a passing thought.

Then, one night in the spring of 1994, I went to—God's honest truth—a toga party hosted by a friend's fraternity. Like my roommates who accompanied me, I went outfitted in a white sheet.

One of the greatest blessings of my life is that Facebook and Instagram didn't exist in the 1990s.

Regardless, off my overweight self went to that toga party—self-conscious, slightly embarrassed, but still hopeful that some boy might take notice.

One did: the very boy I'd secretly admired for months. As I climbed onto the bus that would take us to the party, he looked me in the eye and said, "Wow. I'm surprised you didn't need two sheets."

That was the night I stopped eating.

For the next six years, I counted every gram of fat, every calorie consumed, and every calorie burned. I lost the first twenty-five pounds—the twenty-five pounds I needed to lose—quickly. Then, I lost another twenty-five pounds— twenty-five pounds that I never should have lost. Along with it, I lost my energy, my health, and my thick red hair.

Those losses didn't go unnoticed. My friends threatened to call my parents if I didn't get help. My parents threatened to pull me out of college if I got any thinner. I ignored them all. I didn't have an eating disorder, I assured them; I was just watching my weight.

Never mind that every notebook I owned in college was covered in small columns of numbers, the fruit of my constant tabulation of calories and fat grams, or that a moment of weakness—eating a breadstick or a piece of birthday cake—resulted in hours of tears. My world revolved around the twin axes of food and exercise. I always had a carefully laid plan, accounting for any variations to my daily routine—a dinner out, a coffee with a friend, an interview, or a test. My body, and the little that went into it, were the center of my universe. My body was also, by my way of thinking, my prison, limiting me and controlling me at every turn.

But I didn't have an eating disorder.

"The soul should treat the body as its child, correcting it without hurting it."

St. Francis de Sales

Awakening

The denial stopped during my senior year. One morning, like I did every morning, I stepped onto the scale. The reading was my lowest weight ever. For a moment, I rejoiced. Then, I heard myself think, "It's still not low enough."

That thought startled even me. "What is low enough?" I asked myself.

A more startling thought followed.

"Zero."

Zero. Nothing. Nada. Zilch. That had become the unspoken, unrealized goal of all my eating and not eating. I was going for nothing. I was trying to erase myself, pound by pound, from the world. That's what I wanted: to disappear, to go away, to not exist.

After that morning, with enough time and enough prayer, I came to see that what started out as a diet had become so much more. It had become my coping mechanism—my way of dealing with pain and stress, fear and anxiety. It was how I controlled my world, how I responded to the confusion about my future, God, and the less-than-virtuous choices I saw my friends making all around me.

The eating disorder was also, on a deeper level, my response to my manifold insecurities—insecurities about my appearance, my intelligence, my opinions, really all that made me *me*. I knew I could never be a beauty. Nor could I find a way to shed a few IQ points. And become less opinionated? Not in this lifetime. But I could be small. I could be tiny. And part of me thought that maybe if I looked tiny enough, delicate enough, feminine enough, nobody would mind the strong opinions; they would just disappear amidst the smoke and mirrors of anorexia.

Coming to understand the underlying reasons for my "dieting" eventually helped me see the wrong I was doing to my body and my soul. I recognized, finally, that my behavior was displeasing to God, who made me and loved me. Yet that knowledge didn't change my behavior. Wrong or not, I couldn't stop the counting, weighing, and measuring.

I did try to get better. I'd eat a bit more and gain a bit of weight, only to end up in a panic and return to my old habits. I was terrified of gaining weight. I was terrified of losing control. I begged God for help. But I also begged him to not make me fat again.

FURTHER READING

Weightless: Making Peace with Your Body by Kate Wicker

Cravings: A Catholic Wrestles with Food, Self-Image, and God by
    Mary DeTurris Poust

Bulimia: Hunger for Freedom by Katie Gesto

After graduating from college, I spent the next three years moving in fits and starts closer to "normal." Unfortunately, my first attempts at "normal" eating led instead to binge eating and compulsive over-exercising. Control, for a time, became an all or nothing proposition: I was either completely in control or completely out of control. Then, there was the three-month stretch in 1999 when I abused laxatives. And throughout those years, I tried and failed to be bulimic. Fortunately, for all the hours I spent in bathrooms, hunched over toilets, gagging myself, I never could throw up. I am, for whatever reason, physically unable to vomit.

By November 2000, I looked better. The binge eating episodes brought my weight back up to a healthy number and, although my hair didn't grow back as thick as it was, its waves returned. Mentally, spiritually, and emotionally, however, I was as sick as ever. My eating disorder had come to define me. "Anorexic" was how I saw myself. It was how I believed I would always see myself. Also, even though I ate more, I didn't think any less about food. I still counted every calorie, still parsed every morsel. I hated food, and I hated my body. I wanted to be hungry and I wanted to be lean—gaunt, even—anything but curvy, anything but what I was.

Then, in the last month of the Great Jubilee of the New Millennium, I came back to the Catholic Church.

HOLY ANOREXICS?

What are Catholics today to make of St. Catherine of Siena, who subsisted almost solely on the Holy Eucharist? Or St. Clare of Assisi, who refused food most days of the week? Some historians, looking at Catherine and Clare's behavior, as well as that of other women mystics in the High Middle Ages, have labeled the women "holy anorexics." They see in the women's denial of their bodies a rejection of the body and a rejection of the goodness of the world.

Caroline Walker Bynum, however, in her landmark study *Holy Feast, Holy Fast*, offers an alternate theory to the mystics' extreme ascetical practices. Instead of rejecting the body, Bynum argues that the women were actually embracing the body, particularly its ability to draw them closer to the suffering Christ. Through pain and hunger, they plumbed the depths of the Incarnation.

Moreover, Bynum contends, women chose to renounce food in particular not because eating was problematic, but because food was one of the few goods women had control over during that time. Men could renounce wealth and power. Women, who had neither, could renounce that which they prepared for others: bread, wine, meat, and cheese. While nurturing their families and religious communities with hearty meals, they fasted.

Importantly, Bynum notes, the goal of their fasting was never a slim waistline. The fasting saints didn't desire thinness; they desired holiness. Nor, through fasting, did they seek to control their world. Rather, their fasting was an act of surrender; they surrendered control of their lives to Christ.

In all this, Bynum concludes, "women expanded the suffering, giving self they were ascribed by their culture, becoming ever more wonderfully and horribly the body on the Cross. They became that body not as flight from but as continuation of self."[1]

HOMECOMING

The story of my return isn't nearly as dramatic as that last sentence makes it sound.

Years earlier, about ten months after the onset of my eating disorder, a cute Protestant boy had convinced my badly-catechized self that I had to choose between Jesus Christ and the Catholic Church. In case you didn't know, cute Protestant boys and bad catechesis are a dangerous combination. I gave my life to Jesus in a new way that year, but I also walked away from his Church.

I stayed away for almost six years, still going to Mass occasionally (because I liked the smells, bells, and kneeling), but I no longer considered myself Catholic.

---

[1] Caroline Walker Bynum, *Holy Feast Holy Fast: The Religious Significance of Food to Medieval Women* (Berkeley: University of California Press, 1987), 296.

A few months before my twenty-fifth birthday, however, another cute boy (this time a Catholic) put some questions to me about authority and tradition that I couldn't answer. After that, I did some reading, thinking, and praying, and quite quickly got myself to Confession. And I do mean quickly.

On November 1, 2000, I was a confirmed Evangelical, laughing at a co-worker for believing he needed to go to Mass on All Saints Day, a holy day of obligation. By the time the next holy day of obligation rolled around, December 8, the Feast of the Immaculate Conception, I was kneeling in the third row of my local parish, a daily Mass goer for more than a week.

It was, perhaps, one of the quickest, easiest, and least anguished returns to the Church in history. God was very good to me.

Being me, I spent those first several months back in the Church reading everything I could get my hands on about the Catholic faith. I wanted to make up, in a few short months, for all that I hadn't learned in the first twenty-five years of my life. G. K. Chesterton, Frank Sheed, Peter Kreeft, Karl Adam, and Dietrich Von Hildebrand—in addition to the *Catechism of the Catholic Church* (which I read cover to cover in January 2001)—were my go-to guys back then. I owe them much.

As the weeks went by, their writing, combined with plenty of prayer, began changing my vision of God, the world, and myself. Finally, one day in early March, as I walked back to my pew after Communion, the Eucharist still on my tongue, knowledge became understanding for the first time: "For my flesh is true food and my blood is true drink" (Jn 6:55).

Suddenly, I got it. The most intimate communion I have with God is that I eat him.

I. Eat. Him. He—the almighty, all-knowing, all-loving Creator of the Universe—comes to me as food, as the very thing I feared, as the very thing I hated. And not only does he come to me through the matter I despised, but he also becomes a part of the flesh I loathed. He gives himself to me, body to body, through the act of eating.

That moment changed everything.

RISOTTO CAPRESE

Serves 4

Ingredients

4 ounces pancetta,
   cubed into ½ inch squares

2 tablespoons butter

1 small onion, diced

2 garlic cloves, minced

2 garlic cloves, smashed

1½ cups risotto

½ cup white wine

7-8 cups chicken broth

8 ounces fresh mozzarella,
   shredded or cut into bite-
   sized pieces

½ cup loosely packed basil,
   shredded

2 quarts cherry tomatoes

2 tablespoons olive oil

Kosher salt

Heat olive oil and smashed garlic in a large frying pan; when the garlic turns golden brown, remove from oil; continue heating the oil until it begins to smoke. Toss tomatoes into the hot oil. Stand back—the oil will spit. Once the oil has calmed down, toss the tomatoes to coat. Once they begin to split open, smash with the flat side of a spatula. Cook until all the tomatoes are open and wilted. Salt to taste and set aside.

In a medium saucepan, bring the chicken broth to a simmer (not a boil). In a large pot, melt the butter over medium heat. Add in pancetta and cook until the fat begins to render and the meat crisps. Add in onion and cook until it becomes translucent (about 3–4 minutes). Add in garlic. Cook for 30 seconds or until you can begin to smell the garlic. Then, add in risotto and toss to coat. Cook for one minute, stirring several times as the rice toasts. Add in white wine, and stir until the liquid is absorbed and the risotto begins to hiss. Slowly, stir in one ladleful of broth at a time, being careful not to add more until all the liquid is absorbed. Stir continuously. This should take about 15–20 minutes. When the risotto is creamy and just slightly firm to the bite, remove from heat and stir in tomatoes and cheese. Add basil. Salt to taste (I usually use slightly less than two teaspoons). Serve immediately.

CHAPTER THREE

Reality Re-enchanted
Seeing the World with Catholic Eyes

How did one thought—the thought that eating was the most intimate communion I have with God—undo six years of disordered eating?

It didn't. It wasn't one single thought that brought the healing. It was what gave rise to the thought. It was what all my feverish reading in the months following my reversion gave me: a sacramental worldview.

The word "worldview" can turn a lot of people off. To some, it sounds like something liberal arts professors talk about in college classrooms—interesting, but disconnected from the reality of everyday life. Worldviews, however, are about as egalitarian a concept as concepts come. Everyone has one: the rich, the poor, the educated, the uneducated, the faithful, and the unfaithful. It's how we see the world around us. It encompasses all the assumptions about life that we have, based upon our upbringing, education, faith, and culture.

Those beliefs influence every decision we make and every action we take. Nobody exists in a vacuum. The world in which we're raised influences every one of us. That influence extends to the most minute areas of life: how we dress, how we talk, and, most important for our purposes, how we eat.

AT ODDS

For years, despite my faith, I thought and acted more like a twenty-first-century American than I did like a Catholic. I ate more like a twenty-first-century American than I did like a Catholic. I looked at the world (and myself) the wrong way. I saw food, my body, and the meaning of life itself not with a Catholic, sacramental worldview, but rather with a modernist worldview

If you've read my book *These Beautiful Bones*, you've already gotten a decent primer on the differences between the sacramental worldview and the modernist worldview. I keep coming back to these differences in much of what I write because the concepts are so foundational. It's hard to understand the world in which we live or the world we're called to make if we don't understand the difference between how the culture tells us to see the world and how God wants us to see the world—or, to put it more starkly, between what the culture tells us is real and reality itself.

There is a difference.

AN ENCHANTED WORLD

From Revelation—what God told us in Sacred Scripture and Sacred Tradition—we know that God created the world and everything in it. Every butterfly, every mountain, and every drop of water owes its existence to him. He made it all. Even mosquitoes.

We also know that everything in creation, in some way, reflects its Creator. It says something about him. So, when we see a sunset or a mountain or a mighty river, we know God is glorious, great, and powerful. When rain falls and turns the grass green, we know God gives life. When hummingbirds fly, we know that no detail of creation escapes God's notice; his care extends to the small as well as to the great. And when mosquitoes buzz about? I'm not entirely sure. Perhaps they tell us that God is persistent; he's not going away; he is eternal.

In some ways, we don't need Revelation to tell us these things. For millennium after millennium, men looked to the skies and knew there must be something—or, more accurately, Someone—greater. In sunrises and oceans, they sensed the numinous, the transcendent, the spiritual. It seemed obvious to ancient man that there was more to the world than what he could see.

It seemed equally obvious to ancient man that he was different from the rest of creation; that he was, in fact, above it. He could build more, communicate more, create more, reflect more, give more, and love more. He had gifts, knowledge, and emotions that even the highest creatures couldn't come close to imitating. Beavers could build dams; man could build pyramids.

Man also had the ability to contemplate his experience of those gifts and preserve the fruits of that contemplation for other people and other generations. After a great hunt, deer and boars didn't record their perilous escapes from danger on the walls of caves. Men did.

"Mysticism keeps men sane. As long as you have mystery, you have health; when you destroy mystery, you create morbidity. The ordinary man has always been sane, because the ordinary man has always been a mystic. He has permitted the twilight. He has always had one foot on earth and the other in fairyland."

G. K. CHESTERTON, ORTHODOXY

A SACRED WORLD

What ancient man intuited, God eventually spelled out. He did this by announcing himself to a small tribe of people in the Near East: the Israelites.

God affirmed for them that there was indeed Someone greater, but only one Someone—him, the one true God, not a pantheon of petty gods duking it out in the sky. God also affirmed that he had created everything in the world, and that it was good (mosquitoes included). Most important, he affirmed that man was indeed special. Man didn't just reflect God; man imaged God. He was made in God's image and likeness, just as a son or daughter is made in the image and likeness of their human father. God breathed his spirit into man at the first moment of man's existence, imparting a life to man that was more than human. It was divine.

God also revealed to the Israelites why, for all his goodness and the goodness of creation, things didn't always seem good. Sickness, death, war, destruction—they didn't belong to the original plan. God created man to live in harmony with both him and creation. But, because God wanted man to love him freely, he gave man free will, the capacity to choose between God and self. Man chose self, and in doing so, he chose death.

Actions have consequences. Choices have consequences. And the consequences of our original parents' original sin were, quite literally, life-shattering. Their rejection of God shattered the harmony of creation and deprived them of the life of God in their souls. Our first father and mother still bore his image, but they no longer carried his life within them. When they disobeyed God by listening to the serpent and plucking the forbidden fruit from the tree of the knowledge of good and evil, they lost his gift of sanctifying grace. They lost his gift of sonship.

Each and every one of their descendants inherited that deprivation, that metaphorical hole in their souls. Each of us inherited it. That's why there are crazed wanna-be caliphs chopping off people's heads in the Middle East. That's why there is adultery, divorce, violence, abuse, poverty, hunger, and disease-carrying mosquitoes. That's why there is reality television. Because our first parents lost the divine life that made it easy to love and choose God every day in every situation.

All this is implicit in the Old Testament—in God's initial revelation of himself to ancient Israel. But it took the coming of Jesus Christ, God Incarnate, in the New Testament, to make it explicit.

CULINARY HUMOR AND THE SAINTS

The prize for best cooking quip in Church history goes to St. Lawrence of Rome, a deacon martyred for the faith in the third century. When Lawrence refused to hand over the Church's purse, a Roman prefect had the deacon tied to a spit and slowly roasted to death. Almost miraculously, as his body hung suspended over a roaring fire, Lawrence found the courage to joke with his tormentors: "I'm done on this side. It's time to turn me over."

Maintaining his sense of humor to the end, St. Lawrence's last words were: "I'm cooked through now."

A GRACED WORLD

Through Jesus, the Son of God, we learned that God is One, but also Three—Father, Son, and Holy Spirit, Three Persons sharing one Nature. That nature is self-giving love. We also learned that God wants to invite all people—not just the people of ancient Israel—into his kingdom and family. He wants to give each of us a shot at gaining back what our first parents lost: the gift of divine life.

To make that possible, he established a Church, his Bride and Body on earth. He endowed that Church with teaching authority, to bind and loose in heaven and on earth. And through the Church he gave us the Sacraments: Baptism to impart his life to us, Confession to restore that life when we lost it through personal sin, the Eucharist to sustain his life in us, Confirmation to strengthen it, Holy Orders and Holy Matrimony to help it grow in us, and the Anointing of the Sick to prepare us for life with him in eternity.

Together, Sacred Scripture and Sacred Tradition, both of which have been guarded and handed down to us by the Church, show us a world created by God, loved by God, and governed by God. They show us a world where everything in creation reflects its Creator and where, because of that, everything in creation can become a means of grace, drawing us closer to the One whom it reflects.

The world in which we live is a graced world. It's a world of beauty, wonder, and mystery where God listens to us; where angels guard us and guide us; where human prayers, in heaven and on earth, direct the course of history. It's also a world where matter matters, not because of how much it costs or what it can do for us, but because of the divine truths to which it points, the divine graces it helps convey, and the stamp of the Divine Hand it bears.

In this world, the material and the spiritual are bound up together. You can't separate them because the One who created matter is pure Spirit. His nature is somehow always connected to his handiwork. So, the human person is body and soul; faith is expressed in word and deed; love is a feeling and an action; a fire gives physical warmth but also emotional comfort. You get the picture.

Many people today, though, don't.

"There is a habit that plagues many so-called spiritual minds:
they imagine that matter and spirit are somehow at odds
with each other and that the right course for human life is
to escape from the world of matter into some finer and purer
(and undoubtedly duller) realm. To me, that is a crashing
mistake—and it is, above all, a theological mistake. Because,
in fact, it was God who invented dirt, onions, and turnip
greens; God who invented human beings, with their strange
compulsion to cook their food; God, who at the end of each
day of creation, pronounced a resounding 'Good!' over his own
concoctions. And it is God's unrelenting love of all the stuff of
this world that keeps it in being at every moment."

ROBERT FARRAR CAPON, THE SUPPER OF THE LAMB:
A CULINARY REFLECTION

A MATERIAL WORLD

For a solid millennium—maybe more—most of the men, women, and children living in the Christian West saw the world like I just described it: as a graced home made for man by God and which helped man find his way to his eternal home in heaven. The average Catholic peasant might not have put it that way, but when they knelt down to receive the Blessed Sacrament or looked up at the stars at night, they knew the God they received on their tongue also made the stars at which they gazed. They understood who was God (God) and who was not (man), and they recognized that their eternal happiness depended upon not confusing the two. They knew their place in the divine order, and danced the steps God gave them to dance, seeking to live their faith in the ordinary moments of ordinary days.

The great thinkers and artists understood those truths even more fully, which is how we ended up with St. Augustine's theology and St. Thomas Aquinas' philosophy, Shakespeare's tragedies, Michelangelo's paintings, and Bach's concertos. The glory of grace working in and through nature informed it all.

But slowly, gradually, a different understanding of the world supplanted the sacramental understanding.

Under William of Ockham—a fourteenth-century Franciscan friar—some people stopped thinking of God as a loving father and started thinking of him as an arbitrary despot, who wasn't much better than the mythical gods of old. As Ockham's followers saw it, God didn't command something because it was good; rather, something was good because God commanded it. So, for example, Ockham's followers argued that God didn't say, "Be faithful to your wife" because fidelity is good; instead, they contended that fidelity is good only because God said so. If God had wanted to, they held, he could have declared adultery good or murder a decent thing to do. It was all about God's will, about what he said, not about what was actually good.

As you can imagine, this philosophy encouraged people to stop thinking of God's law as a loving law, a law designed to bring man to his ultimate happiness, and more as something random and arbitrary, something not designed to make man happy, but rather simply to express God's power.

Nobody wants to obey a law that's arbitrary and unloving— nor a ruler who issues those kinds of laws. So, from there, it was just a few short steps (over a few long centuries) to the Enlightenment, which—intellectually speaking—gave God the boot, dismissing faith, prayer, and the sacraments and embracing instead reason, science, and industrial progress.

There is much to be said for reason, science, and progress. To my dying day, I will defend the goodness of indoor plumbing, espresso machines, and optometry, without which I would wander around this earth dirty, tired, and functionally blind. Reason, science, and progress can be good. The problem came in trying to separate those things from God—not allowing faith to illuminate reason, not allowing ethics to guide science, and not seeing progress in terms of holiness, but rather in terms of wealth and material comfort.

That's what happened as the Enlightenment gave way to the Industrial Revolution, which in turn gave way to the Sexual Revolution, the Technological Revolution, and a moral revolution that claimed truth and goodness were in the eye of the beholder, that everything was relative, and (almost) everything permissible.

FOOD MIRACLES IN CHURCH HISTORY:
ST. FRANCES OF ROME

When famine struck fifteenth-century Rome, the city's hungry found a friend in Frances Ponziani. With the help of her sister-in-law and the support of her wealthy husband, Frances fed all who came to her, instructing her servants that they were not to turn anyone away who came to the Ponziani palace begging for food.

Following her orders, the servants distributed corn and wine liberally until Frances' father-in-law learned of her generosity. He ordered Frances to stop. She refused. So, he sold off the family's extra corn and wine, keeping only what the family needed. Frances continued feeding the poor just the same, planning to empty their corn loft rather than allow others to go hungry.

The loft never did go empty, though. On the very day Frances gave away the last kernels, the entire supply was miraculously replenished. The same happened with the wine. No sooner did the family cask run dry, than did new wine mysteriously appear in it, finer and better than before.

After witnessing the miraculous replenishment for himself, Frances' father-in-law reversed course and supported his daughter-in-law's work. Throughout the remainder of the famine, the city's hungry always had friends at the Ponziani palace.

Frances passed away many years later in 1440. The Church declared her St. Frances of Rome in 1608.

AN EMPTY WORLD

With God out of the picture, so was grace. Sunsets were just sunsets, mountains were just mountains, flies were just flies. Nothing spoke of God. Nothing revealed God. Nothing was sacred because of God. Matter—from butterflies to bodies—lost its meaning. Reality became only what we could quantify or measure.

If you could weigh it, see it, touch it, taste it, or put it under a microscope and analyze its various parts, it was real. If you couldn't, it wasn't.

That meant money was real; God wasn't. It meant the body was real; the soul wasn't. It meant earthly success was real; holiness wasn't.

Likewise, with no heaven or hell to worry about, it also meant that a thing's value depended upon what it could do for you in this life. Fast cars and big houses, physical attractiveness and youth, large bank accounts and impressive titles on office doors—those became the currency the culture valued. Not wisdom. Not virtue. Not love of God and neighbor.

Now, fallen man, being fallen man, always had a tendency to value beauty, wealth, and power above faith, hope, and charity. We didn't need a revolution to change that. But the various revolutions of the last several hundred years did make it socially acceptable to say that's what we valued. They normalized sin. They made it normal to care about your body, odd to care about your soul; normal to practice free love, odd to practice chastity; normal to be greedy, odd to give generously.

Moreover, with God out of the picture, so were the limits on what we could do to our body. We could dress it, decorate it, mutilate it, use it, starve it, gorge it, punish it, or pleasure it any old way we liked. That's what follows from rejecting God and embracing a thoroughly modernist approach to life. The body stops being seen as the physical expression of a spiritual soul and becomes just a hunk of flesh, another piece of matter, to do with what we will.

So what does all this have to do with food and my eating disorder?

Pork Tenderloin with Bourbon Sauce

Serves 6

Bourbon makes everything better, including pork.

Ingredients

2½ pounds pork tenderloin

1 cup bourbon

1 cup soy sauce (low sodium)

¾ cup brown sugar

1 teaspoon corn starch

Combine bourbon, soy sauce, and brown sugar. Marinate pork in the liquid overnight or for at least 8 hours.

To make the bourbon sauce, remove pork from marinade, reserving liquid in a small saucepan. Bake at 375° for 45 minutes. Let stand for 10 minutes.

While the pork stands, combine the reserve marinade and cornstarch. Bring to a boil, stirring constantly for one minute or until the sauce thickens, whichever takes longer. To serve, slice the pork, smother with bourbon sauce, and pair with garlic mashed potatoes.

CHAPTER FOUR

Our Daily Bread
Food as Sign and Sacrament

Walking back from Holy Communion on that March day in 2001, I realized for the first time that food wasn't just food. It wasn't simply a combination of fat and calories, vitamins and minerals. Nor was it a mere means to a purely physical end—being thin or fat, healthy or unhealthy, energetic or tired. Food was all that. But it wasn't *just* that.

Like everything in creation, food was also a sign, pointing beyond itself to important truths about man, life, community, and ultimately, God himself.

As soon as I saw that, I stopped thinking about food like a modernist and started thinking about food like a Catholic. I saw food, at long last, through a sacramental prism. And what I saw was beautiful. It was glorious. It was a testimony to God's love, goodness, and generosity.

In an instant, I knew I needed to change. I couldn't keep abusing such an amazing gift. I needed to honor it. I needed to receive it with gratitude. I needed to use it rightly.

Moreover, I didn't just know I needed to do that; I *wanted* to do that. I didn't simply experience an intellectual conversion that day. I experienced a change of heart, a change of desire. I wanted to live in the truth I saw, free from every fear, every compulsion, every ounce of disorder in how I approached food. I wanted to be healed. And in that wanting, in that seeing, I eventually was.

Here, in a little more detail, is what I saw.

FRUIT OF THE EARTH

It starts with one simple truth: food wasn't necessary.

It wasn't. God didn't have to make our bodies in such a way that we needed to be fed morning, noon, and night. He didn't have to make our bodies in such a way that we needed to be fed at all. If he willed it, we could have gotten our nutrition and energy from the sun, the soil, and the rain, like plants do.

God also didn't have to fragment the nutrition we require across multiple food groups or hundreds of different vegetables, fruits, grains, and animals. He could have concentrated it all in one little plant. Kale really could have been the be-all, end-all.

Lastly, God didn't have to make food taste so darned good. The whole lot of it could have tasted like dirt . . . or beets. Yeah, I know, same difference. Still, it could have. Lemons didn't have to taste tart. Arugula didn't have to taste peppery. Bacon didn't have to taste sweet . . . and salty . . . and magical.

But it does. And while an atheist might credit that to the benevolence of random chance, the rest of us know that chance is never that benevolent. Chance might produce beets. But bacon? Not likely.

So, why food? Why the endless, tasty variety of edible goods?

Ultimately, only God knows. There's no book of the Bible that tackles this particular dilemma. He does tell us, however, that, "the tree is known by its fruit" (Lk 6:44). And the "fruit" of eating reveals much.

"[God] likes onions, therefore they are. The fit, the colors, the smell, the tensions, the tastes, the textures, the lines, the shapes are a response, not to some forgotten decree that there may as well be onions as turnips, but to His present delight—His intimate and immediate joy in all you have seen, and in the thousand other wonders you do not even suspect."

ROBERT FARRAR CAPON, *THE SUPPER OF THE LAMB: A CULINARY REFLECTION*

CALLED TO COMMUNION

One of the first and most important fruits of food is community.

God, remember, is a Community. He is a Communion of Life-Giving Lovers, Three Persons sharing everything they have and are with each other from all eternity. That sharing doesn't require any effort on God's part. God gives of himself because that's who he is. It's in his nature. Us? Not so much.

We bear God's image and are called to live in communion with him, but what comes naturally and easily to God doesn't come quite so naturally and easily to us. We must work at being who we are. This life is all about that work. It's about us working at becoming who God made us to be. Food helps us do that.

Our need for food—food that someone has to grow, cook, and store—draws us to one another. It brings us together in cooperation. You eat what I cook. I cook what someone else grew. Someone else grew using seeds that yet another someone else sold.

Even the most self-sustaining farmer/hunter/berry gatherer on the planet, living off grid, slaughtering his own pigs, growing his own wheat, and aging his own cheese still isn't going it alone. He uses tools made by others, recipes developed by others, and techniques honed by others, all passed down to future generations, father to father, mother to mother, YouTube video maker to YouTube video watcher.

As such, each and every step along the food chain, from production to consumption, reflects in some small way the interdependency of mankind. What we eat connects us to others in both the here and now and in generations past and yet to come. It highlights, in screaming neon yellow, that we are made for community. We cannot go it alone.

In a similar way, food brings us together around a kitchen table—three times a day if we're lucky. There, we don't just eat. We talk, laugh, and look one another in the eye. We share stories. We learn about one another. We grow in friendship and love over shared bread. Since the beginning, our need for food has forced us to walk away from our work—from producing—and just *be*, both with ourselves and with others. That's something many of us might not do nearly so often—if at all—if God had designed us to soak up our nutrition from the sun like we soak up Vitamin D.

Moreover, our hunger, which comes upon us with clockwork-like regularity, continuously reminds us that we are not enough. We aren't self-sustaining ecosystems. We are dependent creatures. We need to be nourished. We need to be fed—with food—and with so much more.

"Bodies as incorruptible as diamonds, or bodies lacking in nothing beyond themselves, would have no impulse or orientation toward the world beyond their borders. Waste makes need, and need makes for everything higher than need. Here, in the germ of hunger, is the origin of all the appetites of the hungry soul."

LEON KASS, *THE HUNGRY SOUL:*

EATING AND THE PERFECTING OF OUR NATURE

Gratuitous Love

The "so much more" we need includes comfort, love, healing, and joy. Regardless of time, regardless of culture, food has born those fruits for mankind.

We taste those fruits for the first time at our mother's breast. The comfort of a mother's milk is often the only thing that silences the cry of a newborn babe. As babies grow, they seek out that same comfort again and again: when they're tired, when they're sick, when they're suffering from hurt feelings or bruised bones.

The passage of time brings the same kind of comfort in different ways. Scraped knees are soothed with cookies, bad days at school are forgotten over cups of hot chocolate, and broken hearts are nursed with bowls of strawberry ice cream. Later in life, we offer casseroles as medicine to the grieving, and glasses of wine to those stung by struggles with an ego-tripping boss.

Food gives comfort. It also communicates love. Loving mothers give their breasts to newborns. Then, they give cookies to toddlers, spaghetti to teenagers, and steaks to husbands. When we fall in love, we romance our beloved with fancy meals at home and fancy meals out. When we want to honor our friends on their birthday, we throw a dinner party. And when we want to love Christ by loving the poor, we feed them, dishing out meals at soup kitchens or handing out sandwiches on the street.

Food is a sign of love, in part, because buying it, preparing it, and serving it demands sacrifice. Cakes don't make themselves. Pots of stew don't just appear in a puff of smoke on the table. Cooking always entails work, and that work is an offering—an offering of time, money, and energy.

From that offering comes healing. Good food gives health. Chicken soup gets us over a cold. Oatmeal lowers our cholesterol. Kale smoothies keep our blood pressure low. Even dark chocolate helps us recover from a cough. This alone should be proof positive that God is love.

If it's not, then consider the joy that accompanies good food. As Christians, we don't just celebrate Easter, Christmas, and all the high holy days of the liturgical year by going to church. We celebrate by cooking and eating—sweet honeyed hams and choice loins of beef, garlic mashed potatoes and asparagus wrapped in prosciutto, shortbread cookies and peppermint fudge, pumpkin cheesecake and bourbon-laced eggnog. We feast on these treats and more as an expression of our joy and gratitude. We also feast on them because doing so makes us even more joyful.

Hot buttered rum lifts our spirits and helps put us in the mood for celebrating the birth of God made man. Cinnamon rolls on Easter morning do the same for the Resurrection. They're part of the joy of the season. In that, they're occasions for grace. God works through those tasty treats to help children and adults alike perceive just how special these holy days are. Chestnuts roasting and turkeys filled with stuffing communicate, as clear as any homily does, that this day is not like other days.

As for why God does all this—giving us tasty treats that bring comfort, healing, love, and joy—the most obvious answer is because he is good and because he is love.

God's goodness abounds in every garden and every orchard. Every ripe tomato, every succulent grape, every juicy pear testifies to the One whose words are "sweet . . . to my taste, sweeter than honey to my mouth" (Ps 119:1). They proclaim his goodness in every bite.

Similarly, God's love is manifested in every cocoa bean and every coffee bean, every stalk of wheat and every grain of rice. The endless variety, the limitless combinations, and the delightful tastiness of it all is more goodness than any of us deserve. It's all gratuitous. It's all unnecessary. It's all a complete, unmerited gift. I don't deserve bacon jam. You don't deserve bacon jam. None of us deserve bacon jam. We're weak, foolish, and selfish sinners. But you know what God gives us?

Bacon jam.

He also gives us the Eucharist.

FOOD ON FILM

Not all movies about food are created equally. Some depict food as a substitute for faith (such as *Chocolat*). Others, though, rightly sense the sacramentality of supper and its power to bring grace into people's homes and lives. The films that do that the best include:

- *Babette's Feast,* 1987
- *Pranzo di Ferragosto (Mid-August Lunch)*, 2010
- *Chef,* 2014
- *The Hundred-Foot Journey*, 2014
- *City of Gold,* 2015

BREAD FROM HEAVEN

Nowhere are the bonds between food and the love of God more evident than in the Eucharist.

In the Mass, bread and wine become Body and Blood. In Holy Communion, Jesus Christ gives himself to us as real food and real drink.

The Eucharist is not a symbol of Jesus Christ; it is Jesus Christ. It is the greatest miracle any of us will ever witness and the greatest gift any of us will ever receive. We feed on God so that we can share his life and become what he is.

Food, however, when understood in the light of the Eucharist, is one, big, fat symbol.

Every natural truth about food—food as a source of community, comfort, love, healing, and joy—ultimately points beyond itself to what happens every day in every Catholic church in the world. So . . .

Food creates and sustains community. The Eucharist incorporates us into the ultimate community, the family of God, the Body of Christ.

Food comforts us, making us forget our troubles for a moment. The Eucharist consoles us on an infinitely deeper level, helping us join our sufferings to the suffering of the crucified Christ and exchange our heavy yoke for his much lighter one.

Food signifies love, allowing us to show others how much we care for them. The Eucharist is Love. It's God's complete gift of himself to us.

Food goes hand in hand with sacrifice; it always requires work. The Eucharist is the re-presentation of the greatest sacrifice the world has ever known. It cuts across space and time, allowing each of us to be mystically present on Calvary, where the God of the Universe sacrificed his life for our fallen, broken selves.

Food heals; it strengthens our bodies and our minds. The Eucharist heals too; it heals our souls. It wipes away venial sins and nourishes us with the life of Christ, enabling virtue to grow.

Lastly, food brings joy, but only fleeting, passing, momentary joy. The Eucharist—received frequently, reverently, worthily—brings us the everlasting joy of eternal life with Christ.

Again, the Eucharist isn't the symbol. The symbol is food.

"If [the Eucharist] is just a symbol, to hell with it."

FLANNERY O'CONNOR

BY DESIGN

From the beginning, God knew he would become man and die on a cross. He knew he would give himself to us, body to body, flesh to flesh. The Eucharist wasn't some plan he dreamed up a few thousand years into man's existence. Becoming bread wasn't a scheme he concocted on the fly, after watching the Israelites screw things up one too many times.

God is eternal. He is infinite. He is outside of time. From all eternity, he knew how this whole salvation history drama would play out. Accordingly, food's role in that drama is not a coincidence. It's not happenstance. Food's ability to be both what it is and more than it is, to shed light on natural truths about man and supernatural truths about God, is all by design. God made it that way from the beginning. God always meant for food to be an ordinary sign that would point beyond itself to the extraordinary reality of the Eucharist. God always meant food to be a natural symbol of the very greatest supernatural truths.

This is how the world works. This is reality. This is what a sacramental worldview helps us see. It reveals to us the glory, the majesty, and the mystery contained within a plain piece of bread. It helps us recognize that God wants every meal, every supper, to be a foreshadowing and foretaste of the feast to end all feasts: the marriage supper of the Lamb.

A NOTE ON THERAPY FOR THOSE WITH EATING DISORDERS

When battling an eating disorder, a good therapist is like a Proverbs 31 wife: "more precious than jewels." Therapists can help people understand why they struggle with food and their bodies, as well as learn healthier ways of coping and communicating. A Catholic therapist who understands the sacramental nature of food and can direct their clients to the Eucharist can help even more.

Unfortunately, I was never lucky enough to find a good therapist. If anything, the counseling I received caused more harm than good. Not only did my counselor see my faith as a problem to be overcome, but she also wanted me in a support group, which for anorexics is a crashingly horrible idea. Competitive by nature, most of the girls in my group secretly competed to be the thinnest and borrowed ideas from one another to more effectively starve themselves. Maybe people with different forms of eating disorders can benefit from support groups, but most anorexics need individual, not group, support.

If you or someone you love needs help, however, I recommend contacting the Institute for Psychological Sciences or the Alpha and Omega Clinic, both located in Washington, DC, for possible referrals to solid Christian counselors. I also recommend spending as much time as possible in front of the Eucharist. The grace is real, and without it, full healing is all but impossible.

* * *

Sometimes, when I'm reflecting on my long walk back to my pew in March 2001, it can feel like healing came in an instant, like I walked into Mass with an eating disorder and walked out without one. But it wasn't quite that simple.

It took time for me to shed old habits and learn new ones. It also took time for my body to adjust to healthy eating. All that starving, gorging, and over-exercising did a number on my metabolism, and God didn't repair that damage in an hour. Nevertheless, he still did much of the work that needed doing in me that day at Mass. He gave me a glimpse of the truth about food, and he gave me the desire to live in that truth always.

It wasn't just that one glimpse and that one desire, however, that led me out of the wasteland of anorexia. Just weeks later, God gave me another glimpse, this time of the dignity of the body. And with it came another desire: to care for my body like the temple it was.

Roasted Brussels Sprouts
Serves: 2–4

If you haven't figured it out already, I have a thing for Brussels sprouts. A big thing. My husband does too. We consider ourselves connoisseurs of the tiny little cabbages, and, if you're interested in such things, we can tell you just where to go the next time you're in Pittsburgh to get the best the city has to offer. Most nights, though, we're happy with the basics.

Ingredients

1 pound Brussels sprouts

3 tablespoons olive oil

5 large garlic cloves, peeled and smashed

Pepper and kosher salt to taste.

Preheat oven to 400°. Trim the ends off the Brussels sprouts, then slice in half. On a parchment-lined baking sheet, arrange the Brussels sprouts, flat side down. Scatter garlic cloves in between. Drizzle with olive oil and sprinkle liberally with pepper and salt. Roast for 20–25 minutes or until the bottoms are a deep, golden brown.

CHAPTER FIVE

The Body Beautiful
A Theology of the Body

March 2001 was a big month for me. First came my bolt from the blue insight into food and the Eucharist. Then, just a few days later, came my trip to Catholic University's bookstore in Washington, DC.

I'm a woman who loves her bookstores. I think buying books, new or old, is one of the great pleasures of life. Nevertheless, even for me, bookstore outings don't normally qualify as life-changing events. But this one does.

I remember three things about that day. I remember the weather: it was dark, unseasonably cold, and raining buckets. I remember what I wore: a green skirt and pale blue cotton sweater, a ridiculously inappropriate choice for the cold monsoon raging outside. And I remember the table near the bookstore's entryway: it was covered in books written by then Pope (now Saint) John Paul II.

Among the dozens of books piled high on that table, one in particular caught my eye: *The Theology of the Body*. I'd never heard of such a thing before. A theology of the body? And by the pope, no less? Color me intrigued.

I picked up the book, and, without so much as a glance through its pages, bought it on my way out. If the pope had something to say about the body, if he had any insights into the flesh that caused me so much anxiety and guilt, then it was worth my twenty dollars.

On the list of money well spent in my lifetime, that twenty dollars comes close to the top.

Over the next two weeks, as I slowly made my way through John Paul II's dense, meditative prose, my other reading on the sacramental worldview and the Catholic understanding of matter came into sharper focus. In essence, I saw the pope doing much the same thing as Aquinas, Chesterton, and Belloc. Like them, he explained how the world and everything in it reflected its Creator. He saw everything as a sign, revealing some truth about its Maker, pointing back to its Maker, and giving glory to its Maker.

He focused, however, on one sign in particular: the human body.

SIGN LANGUAGE

In the years since 2001, as the theology of the body has become more widely known in Catholic (and some Protestant) circles, most people have come to associate John Paul II's teachings almost exclusively with the Catholic Church's teachings on human sexuality. John Paul II himself explains, however, that what he gives us in the theology of the body is much more than a discourse on married love. Rather, he gives us an anthropology, a study of what it means to be a human person, made in the image of God.[1]

Using Scripture as his guide, John Paul II reads the human body like the ancients read the skies. He sees it as a witness to its Creator, and he sees foundational truths about both man and God written into every bone, muscle, and pound of flesh. Those truths

---

[1]   John Paul II, *Man and Woman He Created Them: A Theology of the Body*, trans. Michael Waldststein (Boston: Pauline Books and Media, 2006), 185.

can shape how we make love. But they also can shape how we eat, exercise, and do everything we do in these bodies of ours.

Encountering those truths was, for me, as much a part of my recovery from my eating disorder as the Eucharist. They're bound up together, much like Scripture and Tradition. Without both, complete healing would have been impossible.

THEOLOGY OF THE BODY BASICS
St. John Paul II's Theology of the Body

- Was given during the course of 133 Wednesday audiences delivered from 1979 to 1984
- Is an anthropology of what it means to be a human person, a union of body and spirit
- Teaches that the body expresses the person and reveals how men and women are made in the image and likeness of God
- Reveals that the one flesh union of husband and wife points to the life-giving communion within the Trinity
- Shows how using another person for our pleasure violates the dignity of the person
- Calls all human beings to make a gift of themselves to one another in love

---

EXPRESS YOURSELF
One of the most essentials truths that the theology of the body helped me understand was that my body was not a husk, a shell, or a carrying case for my soul. It wasn't, as the modernists would have it, just a hunk of flesh. It wasn't my personal property to manipulate,

use, or dispose of at will. Nor was it a prison, keeping others from seeing or knowing the real me.

Rather, it was the real me.

The body, John Paul II wrote, "expresses the person." It "reveals the living soul." That is to say, our bodies make visible the invisible truths of our inner lives. They allow us to communicate all that we think, feel, and experience. Our bodies make us known in the world.[2]

On one level, this means we communicate happiness with smiles, sadness with tears, and anger with red faces and glaring eyes. Likewise, our thoughts take on flesh with words spoken, eyes rolled, and backs turned. All that would otherwise remain hidden becomes known through the actions, expressions, words, and gestures of our body.

This includes love. We hug our children with our arms, kiss our spouse with our lips, and reassure aging parents with the touch of a hand. We also hear declarations of passion with our ears, smell bouquets offered on anniversaries with our noses, and see eyes that light up in our presence with eyes of our own. Love can't be given or received without the body.

And yes, bodies can become tired and frail. They get sick and grow hungry. But in bodily weakness and vulnerability, God gives us the chance to serve and be served. When our bodies suffer, we can remember that we are creatures, not the Creator. To live we must receive. To exist, we must depend on others. And when the bodies of others suffer, we can remember the God who served us— who healed the sick, fed the hungry, and comforted the afflicted. In that, we're also reminded that he expects us to do the same. He wants us to become like him. That doesn't happen unless we serve like him—selflessly and sacrificially.

---

[2] Ibid., 183.

PATRON SAINTS OF COOKING:

HILDEGARD OF BINGEN

She was born almost four hundred years before the Renaissance began, but that didn't stop St. Hildegard of Bingen from being the ultimate Renaissance woman. A mystic, abbess, scientist, theologian, biblical scholar, gardener, and skilled healer, Hildegard was also a talented (and thoughtful) cook.

Named a "Doctor of the Church" by Pope Benedict XVI, Hildegard's many writings include lengthy passages on cooking and nutrition. She advocated hot breakfasts in the morning, long walks after dinner, and diets rich in spelt, fennel, chestnuts, chickpeas, meat from animals fed grass and hay, certain fruits, and vegetables. She also advised the sisters in her convent against eating strawberries, eel, refined sugar, and sausage.

For all her dislike of sugar, though, Hildegard was a strong believer in the power of cookies. Cookies, she explained, should be eaten often, as "They will reduce the bad humors, enrich the blood, and fortify the nerves."[3]

Clearly, St. Hildegard's designation as a Doctor of the Church was richly deserved.

THE SHAPE OF A LIFE

Our bodies don't just communicate what we think and feel in the moment, though. They also communicate what we've thought and felt in the past. They communicate what we've experienced. They tell the story of us.

---

[3] Gabrielle Uhlein, "Green and Glorious: Meet Saint Hildegard of Bingen," *The Edge*, August 1, 2013, http://www.edgemagazine.net/2013/08/green-and-glorious/.

Laugh lines testify to late nights swapping stories with friends. Stretch marks recall babies brought into the world. Soft curves speak of a love for cheese and wine. Even scars from surgeries and gray hairs have their stories; they bear witness to the darker moments in our lives and lessons learned through suffering.

Similarly, those who have lived hard—who made poor choices regarding how they treated others and themselves—generally end up with bodies that reflect those poor choices. Tabloid images of aging rock stars, corrupt politicians, and starlets desperately clinging to youth remind us of that.

Hatred, vulgarity, cruelty, vanity, pride, self-pity, and insecurity all work their way to the surface eventually. Youth can hide the darkness for a while, but by a certain age, almost everyone has the face they deserve. And even if some have a better face than they deserve, only strangers usually see it that way. Those who know them best look upon them and see the rot in their souls. They see the absence of beauty where there's an absence of love.

Conversely, the bodies of those who've loved hard, who've given themselves away for Christ and for others, grow more beautiful, not less, with the passing of time.

St. Teresa of Calcutta bears witness to that. Everyone who met that tiny, wrinkled old woman walked away from their encounter with her saying she was the most beautiful woman they'd ever met. Her love for God and man was written on her face. In her eyes, they saw mercy. In her hands, they saw compassion. In her shoulders, stooped and bent, they saw humility. Her virtue manifested itself in her every look and action. That didn't just make her soul beautiful. It made her body beautiful. It caused people to see her as lovely. They liked to look upon her.

Again, the body expresses the person. It can't do otherwise.

Divine Witness

The body expresses the person. It also expresses God. As John Paul II explained in his *Theology of the Body*, more so than every other thing and creature in creation, the human body images its maker to the world.[4]

When we create—when we build buildings, paint paintings, compose sonatas, write books, and knit sweaters—we image a God who is the Creator.

When we garden—when we cultivate the soil, sow seeds, water plants, pull weeds, and harvest crops—we image a God who tends to the world and every soul in it, so that his "harvest" will be great.

When we cook—when we bake bread, stir stews, brew beer, and make wine—we image a God who once nourished his people with manna in the desert and now nourishes his people with his Body and Blood in the Mass.

When we serve—when we change diapers for our babies, run errands for our spouses, mow the lawn for our elderly neighbors, or build a shelter for the homeless—we image a God who washed his disciples' feet and hears our every cry for help.

When we suffer—when we turn the other cheek, pray for our enemies, hold back our complaints, and offer our pain to God—we image a God with stripes on his back, a crown of thorns on his head, and nails bored through his feet.

Lastly, when we make love to our spouses—when we give ourselves to another, body and soul, in love, completely, unreservedly, holding no part of ourselves back, including our fertility—we image a God who from all eternity is self-giving, life-giving Love, a Holy Trinity of Persons, a Divine Family, from whom all earthly families take their form.

---

[4] John Paul II, *Theology of the Body*, 151.

The body of every man and every woman is a walking, talking, breathing, laughing, dancing, crying image of God.

The bodies of the baptized are even more. They are temples.

As long as sanctifying grace hasn't been lost through serious, unrepented sin, the Spirit of God dwells in every baptized Christian. This doesn't just make us special. It makes us holy. It makes us sacred. It makes us living tabernacles, the dwelling places of God Most High.

Not surprisingly, that privilege comes with obligations.

"Our Lord does not come down from Heaven every day to lie in a golden ciborium. He comes to find another heaven which is infinitely dearer to him—the heaven of our souls, created in His Image, the living temples of the Adorable Trinity."

ST. THÉRÈSE OF LISIEUX

HONORING THE BODY

One morning, not too long after I first read *The Theology of the Body*, I was at my gym on Capitol Hill doing some exercise or other that I hated—weight training, I think. My goal that morning was the same as every morning: to control my body. I wanted to tame its curves, strengthen its muscles, and tone its softest parts.

Even though God had given me a glimpse of the meaning, purpose, and glory of food, I still saw my body as a problem. I thought of it as a thing separate from me, a thing that needed molding and sculpting and whose value lay in its size.

I wanted to eat well and enjoy food as God intended us to enjoy it. But that desire hadn't taken away the underlying belief that my body's worth was bound up with its appearance. Sure, I knew

God was Love, and food was love. But I couldn't shake the idea that I was only worthy of love if I were thin. And that, I knew, required hours at the gym, taming the flesh, controlling it, molding it, hurting it to "help" it.

That's what motivated me to wake up every morning at 5:00 a.m. and drive across town to my gym, and that's what motivated me on that particular morning in the spring of 2001, as I stood in front of a mirror, checking my form and taming my will . . . which was begging me to call it a day and hit the showers. Like every other morning, the thought, "I have to control my body," ran repeatedly through my head.

Then, suddenly, a new thought answered the old thought. "No, you don't. You have to care for it."

That was the theology of the body talking. It talked good sense.

Caring for the Gift

To control something isn't to care for it. Control is about power. It's about managing a problem. Caring, on the other hand, is about love. It seeks to honor a good. Someone who seeks to control their body and someone who seeks to care for their body are doing two entirely different things. One is treating the body like a problem; the other is treating the body like a gift. One sees the body as a thing; the other sees the body as the person—as me, as you.

When I recognized that, when I stopped thinking of diet and exercise in terms of control and reframed them in terms of care, my attitude and goals shifted dramatically.

I understood that I needed to eat right, nourishing my body with food that was good for me and supplied me with all the energy necessary for the loving and giving God wanted me to do. I also understood that I needed to sleep, not push myself to the point of exhaustion trying to meet my own and others' unrealistic expectations of what a human being can do in a day. And I understood that

I needed to exercise. I needed to move my body, keeping my heart and lungs strong and my muscles flexible.

But I didn't need to be a size two. I didn't need to have visibly ripped arms or washboard abs or buns of steel. I didn't need the body of an elite athlete. I just needed the body of a healthy woman of a certain age blessed with lots of feminine curves.

I also didn't need to make myself miserable doing exercise I hated when I could do exercise I loved. I didn't have to run; I could walk. I didn't have to lift weights; I could do Pilates. I didn't have to darken a gym door ever again if I didn't want to; I could exercise on my own schedule, in my own neighborhood.

God made my body to move, and I understood I needed to move it. That is part of caring for the body. But pushing it to the point of injury and pursuing some completely unrealistic ideal wasn't caring for it any more that not moving it was. Peace and health existed in the balance—not punishing the body like a problem or worshipping it like a god, but caring for it like the temple it is.

"We should love the body insofar as it is obedient and helpful to the soul, since the soul, with the body's help and service, is better disposed for the service and praise of our Creator and Lord."

St. Ignatius

LOVING THE GIFT

Seeing the body as a gift in need of care also helped me appreciate all that my body could do. Exercise became an occasion for praise. I thanked God for movement—for long walks, strong limbs, and the warmth of the sun on my face. I thanked him for lungs that could breathe, a heart that could beat, and eyes that could see trees blooming. I thanked him for every step and every ounce of energy, and in the thanking, exercise became a joy, not a misery.

When I wasn't exercising, I didn't stop praising him. I gave thanks that I could hold babies, who loved nestling up against my soft body. I found hope in the thought that perhaps someday my full hips would help me birth a baby of my own. I started telling God every day how grateful I was that I could appreciate a good Stilton or Bordeaux, that my smile could charm the grumpiest of grocery store clerks, and that my hands, nose, eyes, and mouth could work together to put a meal on the table that would make Julia Child proud.

More than anything else, I thanked God that my body could receive his Body, that it could kneel before him in silent adoration and sing a loud, off-key song. I thanked him that I could smell incense and burning candles, read his story in brilliantly colored stained glass, and tell others about that story by pounding out words on a keyboard.

In sum, I came to love my body because it could love, because it could serve, because it could worship. I came to love my body because it was me. To do anything less was to reject the image of God.

FOOD MIRACLES IN CHURCH HISTORY:
ST. NICHOLAS OF TOLANTINO

When St. Nicholas of Tolantino was around, food behaved in the most extraordinary ways.

Early in his life, the thirteenth-century mystic and future Augustinian friar fell ill. During his sickness, the Blessed Mother appeared to him and promised that if he dipped a piece of bread in water and ate it, he would recover. Nicholas wisely obeyed and was cured instantly. After that, Nicholas urged the same cure on the sick he visited. Similar results followed.

On another occasion, a host who didn't know the friar was a vegetarian served him a plate of roasted chicken. It's said that once Nicholas prayed over the food, the chicken returned to life and flew out the window.

A somewhat less dramatic (if more convenient) miracle occurred under similar circumstances: cooked chicken was set before the saint, he prayed, and instead of losing his dinner to flight, it transformed into roasted potatoes before his eyes.

* * *

I still feel that way. In some ways, my forty-one-year-old body is easier to love than my twenty-five-year-old body. It has loved more and served more in the intervening years. It has also suffered more. That makes it easier to feel more tenderness and compassion towards it. I am more grateful, not less, for what it can do now. This body has served me well.

That's not to say, though, that I never struggle with my body. I do.

I still have days when I wish the face staring back at me in the mirror had a straighter nose and bigger eyes. I also have days when I wish five pounds would magically disappear from my hips and thighs. In a culture that bombards us daily with images of the world's most beautiful women, negative emotions, insecurities, and anxieties about how we look are almost unavoidable.

Nevertheless, thanks to the theology of the body, those bad days are far fewer for me than they would otherwise be. And even when they do occur, they don't get me down for long or trigger any radical behavior. The theology of the body is always in the background, reminding me what matters—God, friends, cheesecake—and helping me enjoy, much more fully, the world God made and the body he created.

What the theology of the body ultimately did was make me free—free to eat, free to cook, free to serve. It enabled me to live the Catholic understanding of food in practical, concrete ways, to make it incarnate in my daily life, and not just know it in the abstract.

What I discovered in Sacred Scripture about food only solidified that freedom.

BACON-WRAPPED, CAJUN-STUFFED PEPPERS
Serves: 5–8

My garden grows an abundance of hot peppers. No matter how dry or wet the summer is, no matter how few or how many pepper plants I put in the ground, I always have more hot peppers than I know what to do with. One summer, we harvested more than two thousand. By August, I'm usually wandering the neighborhood in the evenings, bags of peppers in hand, ready to hand them out to whomever I see. Needless to say, this appetizer is a summer staple. If you come to my house for dinner between July and September, these hotties will be on the menu.

Ingredients
20 Hungarian wax peppers, halved and seeded

8 ounces cream cheese, softened

1 tablespoon Creole seasoning

20 pieces of bacon, cut in half

Toothpicks

Heat oven to 375°. In a small dish, combine creole seasoning and cream cheese. Using a small spoon or butter knife, fill each pepper half with the seasoned cream cheese, wrap with half a slice of bacon, and secure with a toothpick. Place on a parchment-lined baking tray. Bake for 20–30 minutes, or until bacon is completely cooked.

CHAPTER SIX

Bread from Heaven
Food in Sacred Scripture

D uring the six years I spent away from the Church, I picked up a host of good habits that my years of Catholic schooling failed to instill in me. Numbered among those was the regular reading of Sacred Scripture.

These days, I pray Morning Prayer and study the Mass readings. In my Protestant days, I systematically worked my way, back and forth, through the New Testament. (I avoided the Old because I found it confusing.) Nevertheless, despite all that reading, I somehow missed much of what the Bible has to say about food. I knew Jesus fasted for forty days and forty nights (an impressive task to someone as schooled in self-starvation as me), and I did catch the bit about feeding the five thousand with a few loaves and fishes (hard to miss that one). But the rest went right over my head. Blame it on selective reading.

Regardless, when I returned to the Church and began to study the full scope of salvation history—Old Testament as well as New—I was shocked by just how much space the sacred writers allotted to the subject of food.

Food is everywhere in the Bible. From Eden—where man's fall from grace begins with a poorly chosen snack—to Calvary—where

Christ cries out in thirst—salvation history is shot through with references to bread, oil, wine, fig trees, choice roasts of meat, and freshly caught fish. Food is a favorite metaphor in parables, prophecies, and psalms. It's the stuff of miracles in Exodus, Kings, and the Gospels. And, according to Revelation, it's the end to which salvation history leads: the marriage supper of the Lamb is the Bible's closing scene.

In book after biblical book, the sacred authors go back to food again and again. Which makes perfect sense. Man's story can't be told apart from food; it's inextricably woven into the fabric of his life. God's story can't be told apart from food either; God the Son actually becomes food. He becomes bread and wine. Or, more accurately, bread and wine become him.

Salvation history is the story of that becoming.

OUR DAILY BREAD

Food's place in the story of salvation history is, in many ways, ordinary enough. Throughout the Bible, what food is and does isn't all that different from what food is and does in our homes.

In the Book of Psalms, we're told that food comforts: it "strengthens man's heart" (Ps 104:15). In the Second Book of Kings, we see that food heals: a cake of figs fixes King Hezekiah's boil (20:7). In the Gospels and Acts, food nourishes and restores energy: Paul, after his encounter with Christ on the road to Damascus, "took food and was strengthened"; the only advice Jesus gives to the parents of the little girl he brings back from the dead is, "Give her something to eat" (Acts 9:19; Mk 5:43). And in the Book of Ruth, food is the stuff of domestic sacrifice: Ruth feeds her mother-in-law from her own rations, earned by a hard day's work in the fields (2:18).

THE CATHOLIC TABLE   65

In the Bible, food also sits at the center of community and liturgical celebrations: the wedding in Cana involves seven days of feasting; Solomon dedicates his temple with prayers *and* with a feast (Jn 2; 1 Kings 8). Gifts of food, in turn, make friends and win over enemies: bread, wine, and a goat are David's ticket into Saul's household; Joseph's decision to welcome his brothers to Egypt in a time of famine softens their hearts toward him (1 Sam 16:20–21; Gen 45:4–15).

Similarly, food is a gift of kindness, offered to friends and strangers alike: Abraham shows his generosity when he makes a feast for three strangers (Gen 18:2–5); St. Paul instructs that only widows who have shown hospitality may hold places of honor in the community (1 Tim 5:10).

On page after page of Sacred Scripture, food is just ordinary food, doing what food does naturally. In that ordinariness, it helps prove Jesus' humanity. Food demonstrates that he truly is a man. Before the Resurrection, like any man, Jesus gets hungry (Mt 4:2; 21:18). Like any man, he dines with friends and acquaintances (Mk 2:16; Lk 11:37). And like any man . . . well, like some men . . . he cooks: a very manly meal of freshly caught fish on the beach (Jn 21:9). Later, after the Resurrection, on Easter Sunday, in the Upper Room, as the Apostles stare aghast at the Resurrected Jesus, he asks for something to eat, proving to them that he's still flesh and blood, not a ghost or a spirit (Lk 24:41).

Still, for all the ordinariness of food in the Bible, there's plenty of extraordinariness too. Food isn't always just food. Sometimes, it's much, much more.

MEMORIZE THIS

Scripture verses for those struggling with food and
body image.

*"For I, the LORD your God, hold your right hand; it is I
who say to you, 'Fear not, I will help you.'"*
(Is 41:13)

*"For my flesh is food indeed, and my blood is drink in-
deed. He who eats my flesh and drinks my blood abides
in me, and I in him. . . . This is the bread which came
down from heaven, not such as the fathers ate and died;
he who eats this bread will live for ever."*
(Jn 6:55–56, 58)

"Where the spirit of the Lord is, there is freedom."
(2 Cor 3:17)

*"Do you not know that your body is a temple of the
Holy Spirit within you, which you have from God? You
are not your own; you were bought with a price. So
glorify God in your body."*
(1 Cor 6:19–20)

*"For no man ever hates his own flesh, but nourishes and
cherishes it, as Christ does the Church, because we are
members of his body."*
(Eph 5:29–30)

NEAR OCCASIONS

The "more" of food becomes evident at the very beginning of salvation history, when God gives Adam and Eve an earthly paradise filled with good things to eat. He doesn't, however, give them carte blanche to enjoy all that the Edenic smorgasbord has to offer. From the start, God sets up boundaries, warning Adam, "You may freely eat of every tree of the garden; but of the tree of the knowledge of good and evil you shall not eat, for in the day that you eat of it you shall die" (Gen 2:16–17).

The boundary God draws around that particular tree reveals one of the most basic truths about food from the Bible: eating can be an occasion for virtue . . . or an occasion for vice.

In the Garden, food gives man an opportunity to exercise his free will. Through what man chooses to eat, he can obey God or he can disobey him; he can demonstrate his love of and trust in God's will or he can show just how small his faith really is. Essentially, every meal in the Garden becomes an occasion to honor and glorify God or treat him with contempt.

Unfortunately for us, Adam and Eve chose the lesser path, opting for vice over virtue. Humanity has paid the price for that choice ever since.

Later on in salvation history, when God begins the difficult work of turning a "stiff-necked people" into a "kingdom of priests" and a "holy nation," he establishes a new set of boundaries around food (Ex 9:32; 19:6). Only this time, the boundaries are more complicated. In Genesis, it took God one sentence to explain his lone dietary law. In Leviticus, it takes an entire chapter—a very detailed chapter, in which the rock badger, gecko, and stork, among others, are taken off the Israelites' menu—to outline his new dietary plan.

Those boundaries become a defining marker of God's Chosen People. By their refusal to eat swine and rabbit, other nations know them. And when persecution comes in the time of the Maccabees, obedience to the dietary laws gives Moses' descendants an opportunity to prove their love for God. The Greeks demand the Jews eat pig, the faithful Jews refuse, and martyrs are made over a meal: "They chose to die rather than to be defiled by food or to profane the holy covenant; and they did die" (1 Macc 1:63).

With the coming of the New Covenant, God lifts the dietary restrictions of Leviticus (Acts 10:10–15). All is now permissible to eat. There are no forbidden fruits or animals. Bacon can blessedly be enjoyed by all who professed Christ Jesus as Lord. Yet, even with bacon back on the table . . . or more accurately, especially with bacon back on the table, food can still be an occasion for virtue or vice.

The Old Testament opprobrium heaped upon those who ate too much ("Be not among winebibbers, or among gluttonous eaters of meat" [Prov 23:20]) is echoed in the New Testament by St. Paul, who urges the Philippians to imitate him and not the "enemies of the cross of Christ," for "their end is destruction, their god is the belly, and they glory in their shame, with minds set on earthly things" (Phil 3:18–19).

The New Testament likewise heaps the same opprobrium on those who don't share their bacon with others. In Matthew 25, Jesus breaks the news to his followers that whoever refuses food and drink to the hungry and thirsty, in effect, refuses food and drink to him. Such a refusal, he continues, can earn them a one-way ticket "into the eternal fire prepared for the devil and his angels" (vv. 41–46).

In a sense, the lifting of the dietary laws doesn't lessen food's ability to be an occasion for virtue or vice. It heightens it. With greater freedom comes greater responsibility. And with greater responsibility comes greater consequences; namely, hell fire for the gluttonous and the greedy.

"The reason why Christians—and many Catholics—do not understand the Sacrament of the Eucharist as God's sacred feast is because they haven't been well evangelized in the sacramental activity of the family meal. A careful reading of the Hebrew Scriptures through a hermeneutic (or study) of food prepares us for a loftier and more spiritual understanding of the food given to us in the New Testament, namely the Eucharist. But before people can be catechized about that mystery of faith, they must first be evangelized about the commonsense teaching of what food means to us as humans."

Fr. Leo Patalinghug, Epic Food Fight:
A Bite-Sized History of Salvation

Good Provisions

Food's supernatural purpose, however, goes beyond virtue and vice. Scripture also tells us that food is a witness to God: to his existence, his goodness, and his love.

St. Paul tells us this directly in the Book of Acts, "In past generations, [God] allowed all the nations to walk in their own ways; yet he did not leave himself without witness, for he did good and gave you from heaven rains and fruitful seasons, satisfying your hearts with food and gladness" (Acts 14:16–17).

In every crop, in every meal, in every glass of wine, God meant for man to see the hand of a benevolent Creator. Man wasn't supposed to need a prophet or a scroll to tell him that God existed and that God was good. Bread and wine already did that. "Bread is made for laughter," recognized the author of Ecclesiastes (10:19). Wine, echoed the author of Sirach, "has been created to make men glad" (31:27).

The Israelites, however, needed more. They needed God to spell things out. So, he did.

Throughout the Old Testament, God didn't just promise his people that he would provide for them; he promised he would provide the very best. He wouldn't just give them a land of their own; rather, he would give them a land "flowing with milk and honey." Likewise, he wouldn't just feed the Israelites with any old bread; he would feed them "the bread of angels" (Ex 33:3, Ps 78:25). And if they would only obey him, God swore he would reward them with more than a pat on the head; their reward would be "the choicest gifts of heaven above . . . the choicest fruits of the sun, and the rich yield of the months, with the finest produce of the ancient mountains, and the abundance of the everlasting hills" (Deut 33:13–15).

Later, in the New Testament, God the Son did what God the Father promised. At Cana, he turned dirty water into the finest wine. "Every man serves the good wine first; and when men have drunk freely, then the poor wine," said the astonished steward to the bridegroom, "but you have kept the good wine until now" (Jn 2:10).

Afterwards, first on a mountaintop and later on a plain, Jesus turned a few loaves of bread and a couple of fish into feasts for thousands. "And when they had eaten their fill, he told his disciples, 'Gather up the fragments left over, that nothing may be lost.' So they gathered them up and filled twelve baskets with fragments from the five barley loaves, left by those who had eaten" (Jn 6:12–13).

In both the Old Testament and the New, food's abundance and tastiness signify God's favor. It is a natural sign that helps the Jewish people understand that God is good and God is love. It also helps them understand that this good, loving God loves them. They can trust him. He will not lead them astray.

But what about when food isn't abundant or tasty? That signifies something too. It signifies that something is amiss.

Egyptians, who kept the Israelites enslaved for centuries,

watched their food supply dry up when Pharaoh refused to let God's people go: "He smote their vines and fig trees, and shattered the trees of their country" (Ps 105:33). Centuries later, famine preceded the fall of the disobedient Kingdom of Israel to the Assyrians and the fall of the equally disobedient Kingdom of Judah to the Babylonians (Lk 4:25; Jer 52:6).

The Book of Revelation foretells similar problems about the end of days: "And behold, a pale horse, and its rider's name was Death, and Hades followed him; and they were given power over a fourth of the earth, to kill with sword and with famine and with pestilence and by wild beasts of the earth" (6:8).

God makes the rain fall on the just and the unjust. Good harvests come to sinners, and famines take the lives of saints. But what Scripture helps us see, in large, bold print, is that an abundance of food reflects how the world was supposed to be: it reveals the goodness and generosity of God, a goodness and generosity that would have manifested itself always and everywhere if man hadn't fallen. Likewise, a shortage of food is a result of sin—maybe not individual sin, but at the very least Original Sin. Famine and hunger are the lot of a fallen, broken world. A barren land is a physical manifestation of a world without grace and without God.

FEEDING THE HUNGRY

For those who seek to follow Christ, it's never enough to simply satisfy the needs of our bellies. Our faith obligates us to feed the hungry and provide drink to the thirsty. If we do that, Christ promises us eternal life (Mt 25:23). If we don't, he warns of "eternal punishment" (Mt 25:46).

Serving Christ by serving his hungry poor doesn't require food miracles on the scale of St. Frances of Rome. It simply requires an attentive eye and a generous heart.

Here are some easy ways to follow Christ's command to feed the hungry:

- Volunteer at a soup kitchen or homeless shelter.
- Donate money or food items to a food pantry.
- Support an organization that feeds victims of famine, war, and systemic national poverty.
- Make a meal for a family with a new baby.
- Invite a young family or a person who lives alone to join you for dinner.
- Keep gift certificates to a fast food restaurant on hand to give to the homeless.

SAVING BREAD

There is still yet another meaning to food in both the Old Testament and the New. It is the ultimate meaning, the ultimate divine sign: food saves. Salvation, first for the Israelites and then for the whole world, is made possible through a meal.

In Genesis, every time God makes a covenant with his people—every time he invites them into an enduring familial relationship with himself—food plays a role.

Food is in the Garden at Creation, when God makes his first covenant with Adam and Eve; what foods Adam and Eve cannot eat (the fruit from the tree of the knowledge of good and evil) is the law of that first covenant, the condition the first couple must obey if they want to honor their relationship with God.

Food is also part of God's covenant renewal with Noah: he gives Noah permission to eat not just the fruit of the earth, but also the creatures of the earth.

When God makes his covenant with Abraham in Genesis 15, he requires a ritual meal of sorts, with animals split in two and a smoking pot.

Generations later, the importance of food at which earlier covenants only hinted becomes even more evident when God explains to Moses his plan to save the Israelites from slavery: He tells them to take a lamb, slaughter it, and spread its blood on their doorposts. Then, they must roast it—not boil it or serve it raw, but roast it. God gets very specific about that part.

Once roasted, they must eat the lamb with unleavened bread and bitter herbs, loins girded, ready to flee. If they do as God commands, if they carry out the terms of this ritual meal to the letter, God promises to spare their firstborns from the tenth and final plague.

And he does. The Egyptians' children die, the Israelites' children live, and Pharaoh finally relents: the Israelites are free to go. For them, a sacred meal becomes the means of salvation from slavery. Eating leads to freedom. It is their ticket to a new life. It is a mechanism for deliverance.

Centuries later, when the Israelites are finally established in the Promised Land with a king of their own (David), food becomes not so much a mechanism for deliverance, but a means of expressing thanks for deliverance. Following David's lead, when someone is rescued from dire straits, they make fast for the temple, where they offer a bloodless sacrifice of bread and wine. They then eat that bread and drink the wine with their families, expressing thanks for their deliverance. That sacrifice was called the *todah*, which meant "thanksgiving." In Greek, it translated to *eucharistia*.

> *"God becomes the cook, the host, and the food itself in this Eucharistic banquet."*
>
> ANGEL F. MENDEZ-MONTOYA, *THE THEOLOGY OF FOOD: EATING AND THE EUCHARIST*

THE LAMB'S SUPPER

Both the Passover and the *todah* foreshadow an entirely different kind of meal, a meal that is both a means of salvation and a thanksgiving for salvation.

Jesus first speaks of this meal in John 6, telling disbelieving crowds that his flesh is real food and his blood is real drink. He also warns, "Unless you eat the flesh of the Son of Man and drink his blood, you have no life in you" (v. 53). Calling himself "the living bread which came down from heaven," he promises, "if any one eats of this bread, he will live for ever; and the bread which I shall give for the life of the world is my flesh" (v. 51).

Jesus loses countless followers that day. The crowds dismiss him as mad. But on the night before he dies, he explains to his most faithful followers, the Twelve who stayed, how this will be possible.

In the Upper Room, he takes bread, breaks it, blesses it, and speaks the words that will forever after turn bread into body: "This is my body which is given for you. Do this in remembrance of me" (Lk 22:19).

He next takes a cup of wine, saying, "This cup which is poured out for you is the new covenant in my blood" (Lk 22:20).

Then, the next day, he offers his body and pours out his blood on Calvary, uniting meal to sacrifice and making them one.

Just days later, on the first Easter Sunday, after Jesus appears to the Twelve in the Upper Room he appears to two followers on the road to Emmaus. Although he walks with them for miles, they don't recognize him until he again "took the bread, blessed it and broke it and gave it to them" (Lk 24:30).

In that instant, as bread becomes body once more, Jesus disappears from their sight. The disciples, however, don't need him physically present to know him: "he was known to them in the breaking of the bread" (v. 35).

For two millennia, the successors of the Apostles and their helpers have repeated the words Jesus spoke on that first Holy Thursday and first Easter Sunday, blessing bread and wine in the Holy Mass. And when they do, by a miracle of grace, the Holy Spirit changes the very substance of the bread and wine, so what priests offer isn't wheat and grapes but the same flesh and blood offered in the Upper Room and sacrificed on Calvary. It is the Holy Eucharist. And like those first disciples, we too are called to recognize Christ's saving presence in the breaking of the bread.

The Eucharist is the New Passover: a sacrificial meal that delivers all who partake in it from death. It is a meal that brings salvation, imparting not simply new life, but the life of God—sanctifying grace—into the soul. It is the entry point to eternal life.

The Eucharist is also the New *Todah*, a sacrifice of thanksgiving, where the occasion of our salvation is not only recalled but re-presented, made present again in time, and where all who receive it do so with a great Amen—an enduring Yes to God, faith, and life.

In the Letters of Paul, we see the New Passover, the New *Todah*, at the heart of the early Church's life. It's why the first Christians gathered together. It's what they did when they gathered together: they ate a meal. They ate the Lord's Supper. They ate the Lord himself (1 Cor 11:18–34).

The Church on earth, however, isn't the only one participating in that divine meal. As Revelation tells us, the saints in heaven dine right along with us: "And the angel said to me, 'Write this: Blessed are those who are invited to the marriage supper of the Lamb.' And he said to me, 'These are true words of God'" (Rev 19:9).

Eating the Lord's Supper is what all the blessed do in eternity and what God calls each of us to do, both now and at the end of our earthly days. He calls us to bow before the Lamb who was sacrificed, sing out our Amens and Alleluias, and participate in the marriage supper of the Lamb, the supper that saves.

* * *

In some ways, the Bible is the ultimate cookbook. It doesn't include a lot of recipes—although you will find a few. What it lacks in cookery advice, however, it makes up for by helping us understand the "why" of eating. It testifies to food's sacramental value as a sign of God's goodness and as a means of grace. It also shows us food actually becoming grace at the Last Supper.

What Scripture shows us is beautiful—glorious even. It shows us a universe teeming with abundance, love, and life in the form of bread and wine, olives and figs.

This beauty, however, raises a question: If food is so glorious, if it's such a great gift, then why does the Bible also talk so much about forgoing that gift, about renouncing food and going without? And why do the Church's popes, saints, and laws call us to do the same?

In short, if God made us to eat and eat well, why do we fast?

Lamb & Sweet Potato Stew
Serves 4–6

I've shared this recipe on my blog before, but a book about food and the Eucharist didn't seem complete without a lamb recipe. And this is the best one I have.

1½ pounds of lamb shoulder, bone-in

8 ounces white button mushrooms, sliced

2 15-ounce cans of diced tomatoes

1 large sweet potato, peeled and roughly chopped

4-5 tablespoons olive oil

2 tablespoons sugar

Kosher salt

½ tablespoon Cajun seasoning

4 cloves garlic, peeled and lightly smashed

fresh rosemary (optional)

Ingredients

In a large pot, heat 2 tablespoons olive oil over medium-high heat. Once hot, add in the lamb shoulder. Brown on both sides (about 2–3 minutes per side). Add in tomatoes, using the juices to scrape up any browned bits on the bottom of the pan. Stir in the sliced mushrooms, sugar, and about 1 teaspoon of salt. Reduce heat to low. Cover and simmer for two hours.

When the stew is about 30 minutes from completion, pre-heat oven to 400°, line a rimmed baking sheet with parchment paper, spread out the sweet potatoes and smashed garlic, drizzle with remaining oil, and season with Cajun spices. Bake for 20–25 minutes or until the potatoes are tender and lightly browned.

After the meat has simmered for at least two hours, remove the lamb from the pot and separate the meat from the bone. The meat should be falling off the bone. Cut the meat into bite-size pieces, then return to the pot, discarding the bones. Add in roasted sweet potatoes and check seasoning to taste, adding more salt or sugar if desired. Before serving, garnish with a sprig or scattering of fresh rosemary.

CHAPTER SEVEN

Holy Fast
Hungering for Christ

To fast or not to fast? That was the question.

In February 2002, I'd been back in the Church for over a year and eating more freely for a solid eleven months. I'd also changed addresses. Two months earlier, I'd left my job in Washington, DC, and moved to Steubenville, Ohio, to begin graduate studies in theology at Franciscan University.

That month, in Steubenville, the pious masters students who surrounded me were preparing for Lent. Some planned to give up chocolate. Others coffee. A few had vowed to go without meat until Easter Sunday. But what would I do?

During the previous year I'd read enough to understand the importance of fasting. All the great Catholic spiritual masters sang its praises. The saints, almost without exception, fasted with gusto. I wanted to fast with gusto too. I'd spent years denying myself for the sake of the numbers on the scale; now I wanted to deny myself for the sake of my soul.

A wise friend, who knew my history, urged caution. I didn't listen.

Instead, I opted for a progressive fast. I planned to start small
and increase my penances as the weeks went by. Visions of a humble, gentle Emily spending Holy Week meekly dining on vegetables
and water danced through my head. I was confident it would be the
best Lent ever.

Not quite.

For the first week of my fast I gave up sweets. No sweat. The
second week I fasted from sweets and meat. Easy peasy. By the third
week I was off sweets, meat, and dairy. That proved more challeng-
ing. The next week I said goodbye to coffee . . . and joy. The week
after that wheat went off the menu . . . and the rest of my sanity
disappeared. By the time Good Friday arrived I was eating like a
tee-totaling, vegan Mormon celiac on a diet. Or, to put it more accurately, I was eating like a miserable, crabby, horrible wench of a
tee-totaling, vegan Mormon celiac on a diet.

That was a special year for everyone.

Lent 2002 was, in short, a crashing, burning, banging wreck.
And I was an even bigger crashing, burning, banging wreck. I didn't
relapse into anorexia, but I missed the purpose of the Lenten fast
just the same.

FASTING: A SHORT HISTORY

For the better part of the last two thousand years, followers of
Christ have denied themselves food and drink in order to atone
for sins, grow in virtue, and draw nearer to Christ. If you wanted
to become holy, fasting from actual food (as opposed to generic
concepts such as "indifference") was considered a must. No hungry,
no holy.

Christians, however, didn't come up with that idea all by themselves. Since time immemorial, the spiritually-minded across the

globe have freely chosen to go without sustenance for the sake of interior growth.

Long before Moses appeared on the scene, Egyptian men abstained from food as part of their priestly formation. Later, on the other side of the globe, the Incas fasted to appease their gods. In ancient Greece, the pagan philosophers practiced and preached culinary asceticism, believing that forgoing food purified the body. And, in the Far East, before the Buddha became Buddha, he dined daily on one grain of rice and a lone sesame seed, hoping his fast would further his search for enlightenment.

The Christian practice of fasting drew most directly from the ritual fasting of our spiritual ancestors: the Jews. The Book of Job, one of the oldest books in the Bible, recounts the woebegone Job rending his garments and abstaining from food while he mourned the loss of his family and fortune. In the Book of Exodus, Moses fasted for forty days and nights as he prepared for his mountaintop encounter with the Lord (Ex 34:28). And in the Book of Leviticus, God himself instructed the Israelites on the importance of fasting as a means of atoning for sins. He did that by calling for an annual Day of Atonement (Yom Kippur), on which Israel as a nation would fast in reparation for their transgressions (see chapter 16).

In the centuries (and biblical books) that followed, Israel's kings, soldiers, prophets, and priests fasted for those same reasons. They fasted when they mourned (See Judg 20:26; 2 Sam 1:12). They fasted to prepare for some great event (See 2 Chron 20:3; Esther 4:16). And they fasted to atone for their sins (See 1 Sam 7:6; Ex 9:5).

> *"I strive every day against concupiscence in eating and drink-*
> *ing; for this is not the sort of thing that I can decide to give*
> *up once and for all and never touch again, as I was able to do*
> *with sex. Therefore I must keep a hold which is neither too*
> *loose nor too tight on the bridle of my throat. And it is scarcely*
> *possible, Lord, not to be carried slightly beyond the bounds of*
> *necessity. Anyone who can keep exactly within them is a great*
> *man and greatly should we praise your name. But I am not,*
> *since I am a sinful man."*

ST. AUGUSTINE, CONFESSIONS

THE CHRISTIAN FAST

Jesus Christ was born into that culture of fasting, and he made it his own. In obedience to the Law of Moses, he kept both the feasts and fasts of his people (Mt 5:17). Before beginning his public ministry, he fasted forty days and nights in the wilderness (Mt 4:2). He also fasted as he hung on the Cross—hungry and thirsty—atoning for the sins of the world (Jn 19:28).

During Jesus' earthly life, his followers feasted more than they fasted. But, as Jesus predicted, once the Bridegroom was no longer in the disciples' midst, their season of fasting began (Mt 9:14–15).

The Book of Acts tells us that Saul fasted for three days following his encounter with the Risen Christ on the Road to Damascus (Acts 9:9). Later, it recounts the Apostles fasting before making important decisions and choosing leaders (13:3; 14:23). A century later, the *Didache*, a collection of the teachings of the twelve Apostles, counseled Christians to fast on Wednesdays and Fridays every week. Also in the second century, Christians began fasting for several days before Easter.

By the fourth century, those several days expanded exponentially with the emergence of Lent. Other days of communal fasts soon worked their way into Christians' liturgical year, including Advent, Ember Days, and vigils preceding great feasts of the Church.

Even when the whole Church wasn't fasting, individual Christians were, with many of the Desert Fathers existing only on raw vegetables and a select group of medieval mystics subsisting on the Eucharist alone.

Most religious communities counseled less extreme measures, but the forsaking of meat, animal products, and cooked food, not to mention wine, sugar, and other luxuries, was par for the course in monasteries and convents for many a long century.

Food Discipline

Fasting doesn't have to mean forgoing all food but the Eucharist and the occasional berry. It also doesn't have to be confined to Lent. Almost anyone can take on these simple food-related penances almost any time of year:

- Save sweets for Sundays and feast days.
- Abstain from alcohol during the week.
- No snacking.
- Avoid putting extra salt on your food.
- Drink your coffee black or without sugar.
- Forgo buying expensive wines or beers.
- Eat all the leftovers in your fridge.
- Eat whatever you're served.
- No second helpings.
- Choose to cook/eat one food each week that you do not like.

- No eating out.
- No fast food.

HOLDING FAST

Today, however, despite its noble lineage, fasting has fallen on hard times. Ember Days went the way of the 1962 missal, and vigil fasts did the same. On Sundays gone by, Catholics' pre-Communion fast started at midnight. After Vatican II, it started a mere one hour before Holy Communion. Around the same time, abstinence from meat on Fridays became just one optional penance among many for Roman Catholics. Now, fasting from food is in decline even during Lent, with increasing numbers of Christians opting to fast from Facebook rather than sweets and giving up gossip (which you're not supposed do any time of year) in lieu of beer and booze.[1]

Plenty of Western Christians still do go without food on occasion. We embark upon Juice Fasts and Green Cleanses and 21-Day Fixes. But those are diets, not spiritual fasts. When it comes to food, our bouts of self-denial are usually about the body—rarely about God.

COMMON OBJECTIONS

Part of the reason for fasting's waning popularity is simple confusion.

Some people conflate fasting and dieting. They look back on their experiences of restricting calories—of blood sugar crashes,

---

[1]   Anne Stricherz, "10 New Valuable Ways You Can Fast During Lent," Servant of God Cora Evans (blog), February 16, 2016, http://www.coraevans.com/blog/article/10-new-valuable-ways-you-can-fast-during-lent; Father Alberto Cutie, "Lenten Journey," *Huffington Post*, May 12, 2012, http://www.huffingtonpost.com/father-alberto-cutie/lenten-journey_b_1339020.html; Elizabeth Koessler, "During Lent: Feast, Don't Fast," Diocese of Montreal Website, accessed May 21, 2016, http://www.diocesemontreal.org/blogues/en/during-lent-feast-dont-fast/.

"hangry" breakdowns, and unproductive days at work—and wonder how anything good could come of repeating the experience.
Others reject fasting due to a mistaken understanding of why
Christians fast, thinking that the Church's endorsement of fasting
is a rejection of the body or food. They (rightly) reject those ideas,
and (wrongly) reject fasting along with them.

More fundamentally, though, much of the reticence regarding
fasting has to do with living in a land of plenty.

In a society teeming with luxuries, many of us have grown soft.
We don't want to be hungry. We don't want to be uncomfortable.
We don't want to say no to something good. Nor do we have much
practice in saying no to something good. Indulgence, not self-denial, is the law of the land.

In his book *We Have Met the Enemy: Self-Control in an Age of
Excess*, Daniel Akst unpacks the consequences of living in a country that he likens to "a giant all-you-can-eat buffet, one that offers
more calories, credit, sex, intoxicants and just about anything else
we can take to excess than at any time in history."[2]

The result, he concludes, is a populace unable to say no to the
smorgasbord's offerings. "We may vow, as we load up our plates, to
start on a diet tomorrow," he writes, "but tomorrow the buffet is
still there. And when tomorrow comes, we're still hungry."[3]

On yet another level, many people, even Catholics, reject fasting because of the effects of the materialism we talked about in
chapter 3: Modernism led some to embrace a form of Gnosticism
which denies the importance of the body. This kind of Gnosticism
tells us that only the spiritually weak and immature fast from food;
the spiritually mature know there are more important things from
which to fast.

---

[2] Daniel Akst, *We Have Met the Enemy: Self-Control in an Age of Excess* (New
     York: Penguin, 2011), 7.
[3] Ibid.

Giving voice to that sentiment, one Catholic commentator, advocating for a fast from "indifference," recently explained, "If you want to change your body, perhaps alcohol and candy is the way to go. But if you want to change your heart, a harder fast is needed."[4]

Echoed another, who was urging Catholics to bike to work during Lent, "Let's face it, no one stands to benefit from you depriving yourself of chocolate for six weeks (yet again), and the climate needs all the help it can get."[5]

These commentators, however, have it all wrong . . . at least if two thousand years of Church teaching is to be believed.

> "God has given us the goods of the earth, not only that we may enjoy them, but also that we may have the means of . . . showing him our love by the voluntary renunciation of his gifts, and by the oblation of them to his glory."
>
> St. Alphonsus de Ligouri

SPIRITUAL STRENGTH TRAINING

Unlike the culture, the Church doesn't see the body and soul as two completely separate entities. She knows they don't exist in isolation from one another; in this life, the two are inextricably linked. The soul animates the body. The body expresses the soul. Contrary to the famous quote, often misattributed to C. S. Lewis ("You don't

---

[4] Christopher Hale, "Pope Francis' Guide to Lent: What You Should Give Up This Year," *Time Magazine*, February 18, 2015, http://time.com/3714056/pope-francis-lent-2015-fasting/.

[5] Clara Chaisson, "When in Rome: For Lent, Catholics Are Fasting for Climate Change," National Resources Defense Council, February 21, 2015, https://www.nrdc.org/onearth/when-rome.

THE CATHOLIC TABLE   87

have a soul. You are a soul. You have a body."), the Church teaches
that the soul doesn't "have" a body, and the body doesn't "have" a
soul. You are your body. Your body is you.[6]

As we discussed in chapter 5, that intimate, inseparable earthly
relationship means that what our souls do shapes our bodies, and
what our bodies do shapes our souls. You can't live a life filled with
anger, hatred, greed, and envy and not have it reflected in your
body in some way. Likewise, you can't go around committing acts
of violence or lust with your body and not have it affect your soul.
What happens on the inside works its way outward, and what happens on the outside works its way inward.

For this reason the Church has always seen fasting primarily as
a spiritual practice. It may involve the body, but it's the body doing
something for the sake of a healthier soul, not a slimmer waistline.
The Church really does teach that giving up chocolate for Lent
can change us. It also teaches that giving up meat every Friday can
make the world a better place.

It teaches that for several reasons.

First, fasting can change us (and, in turn, the world) because
it helps us grow in virtue. Thanks to Original Sin, our reason and
our desires are not always in perfect accord. Fallen humans have
a bad habit of wanting what we shouldn't want or wanting what
we should want, but wanting it at the wrong time. The reasonable
thing is to deny those disordered desires . . . but few among us always do the reasonable thing. Thank you, concupiscence.

Fasting, however, helps us learn to put reason where it right-
fully belongs: in charge. It forces us to flex our spiritual muscles
and grow stronger as we resist temptation in the form of a gooey
piece of German chocolate cake. Muscles toned by controlling one

---

[6]   The actual quote is from the novel *A Canticle for Leibowitz* by Walter M.
Miller, Jr. The C. S. Lewis Foundation has repeatedly denied that Lewis said
any such thing. Lewis was smarter than that.

appetite—hunger—can then help us control other appetites: anger, revenge, greed, praise, power, pleasure, and lust.

"It is impossible to extinguish the fires of concupiscence," wrote the monk John Cassian in the fifth century, "without first restraining the desires of the stomach."

Or, as a wise old priest once told my husband: "Cookie today; woman tomorrow."

The Spirit of a Pleasing Fast

While the Church's practical rules for fasting have softened through the centuries, the spiritual rules have not.

First, we must not make a fuss about fasting: "When you fast, anoint your head and wash your face, that your fasting may not be seen by men . . ." (Mt 6:17).

We also must not think of fasting as a one-way ticket to holiness, because, as St. John Chrysostom warned, "Christ did not say, 'Come to me because I fasted . . . ,' but 'because I am meek and humble of heart.'"[7]

Then there's the need to be wary of any creeping legalism—putting voluntary penances before charity or putting the letter of the law before the spirit of the law. St. Thomas Aquinas had some particularly strong words for Christians who abstained from what the Church mandated they not eat (i.e. meat on Fridays), but ate otherwise sumptuous meals on fast days.[8]

And unless Christ has personally shown up to betroth himself to you (á la St. Catherine of Siena) or you've taken to a nunnery and are under obedience to superiors, it's generally unhealthy and unwise to put yourself in contention for fasting

---

[7] Walker Bynum, 38.

[8] Thomas Aquinas, *Summa Theologica*, II-II, q. 147, a. 8.

events in the Spiritual Olympics. You can give up sweets during the week without the permission of a spiritual director, but if you're tempted to live off bread and water for a month or forgo animal products for the rest of your days, first run the idea by someone more spiritually sober than you.

FRINGE BENEFITS

In addition to helping us grow in virtue, fasting from food has the added benefit of freeing up resources—whether food or money—for the poor. Forgoing our daily cinnamon dolce latte leaves us with extra cash to give to the soup kitchen around the corner. Eating only half of our dinner at the fancy new steakhouse leaves us with a box full of leftovers to share with the homeless man standing outside. Moreover, as St. Augustine explained, when we fast so that others might eat, not only do our neighbors benefit from our charity, but so does Jesus Christ. "The hungry Christ will receive that from which the fasting Christian abstains," he wrote.[9]

Fasting is also a powerful spiritual weapon against evil. Jesus told us some evils could only be overcome "through prayer and fasting" (Mt 17:21). The Church takes him at his word.

Exorcists fast before casting out demons. Popes, including most recently Pope Francis, have called for fasting in times of war.[10] Even the American bishops, in their fight to protect religious liberty, have asked Catholics to fast.[11] They understand that fasting

---

[9] Walker Bynum, 35.

[10] "Pope Calls All Catholics to Pray and Fast for Syria on Saturday," *Catholic Herald*, September 3, 2013, http://www.catholicherald.co.uk/news/2013/09/03/pope-calls-all-catholics-to-pray-and-fast-for-syria-on-saturday.

[11] John Westen, "Pray, Fast, to Protect Life, Religious Liberty: U.S. Bishops Launch New Campaign," *Lifesite News*, December 6, 2012, https://www.lifesitenews.com/news/pray-fast-to-protect-life-marriage-religious-liberty-u.s.-bishops-launch-ne.

adds an urgency and power to our prayers; it makes our prayers more powerful. It does that by bringing the whole person into the prayer, so we're praying not just with our hearts and minds, but with our bodies. It is, in a sense, a consecration of the whole person to a particular prayer. God responds to that.

Fasting also gives us a concrete way to atone for our sins. After King David slept with Bathsheba and killed her husband, he knew that a simple "sorry" wouldn't suffice. It wasn't enough to just apologize to God; he needed to do something to show God how contrite and chastened he felt. In some tangible way, David needed to atone for his sin. So, he fasted. The Church calls us to imitate him by fasting in sorrow for the evil we've done. Penitential fasting isn't a punishment; it's a gift. It's an opportunity to atone for what we did wrong.

Through it all, fasting helps us remember who we are: weak, frail, hungry men and women dependent upon God's grace. When we fast with a mind for God, and not ourselves, the hunger we experience reminds us of our fundamental neediness not just for food, but ultimately for God. That God is a God who hung from a cross, hungering in body and soul, for our salvation. He hungers for that still. Through our hunger, we can find the One who hungers for us.

Pope Benedict XVI explained, "Denying material food, which nourishes our body, nurtures an interior disposition to listen to Christ and be fed by his saving Word."[12]

That, ultimately, is why the saints of yesteryear embarked on such great fasts. Not to prove how holy they were, but to become holy, to draw nearer to the hungry, suffering Christ through their own hunger, and in that nearness become more like him.

---

[12] Pope Benedict XVI, "Message for Lent 2009," December 11, 2008, http://www.vatican.va/holy_father/benedict_xvi/messages/lent/documents/hf_ben-xvi_mes_20081211_lent-2009_en.html.

* * *

All those years ago, during my first foray into fasting, I didn't understand that purpose. I didn't see fasting as a way to grow closer to Christ. I saw my ability to Sacrifice All the Things as a way to prove my personal holiness. For six weeks, my fast had been all about me—about me doing something big for God.

Moreover, I powered through that fast just like I powered through six years of anorexia—by the sheer force of my will. I didn't pray. I didn't allow my hunger to draw me closer to God. I didn't even ask God what he wanted from me that Lent. I just fasted like a mad woman . . . and everyone else paid the price.

After that Lent, I did some serious thinking about what went wrong. I also decided to follow my friend's advice and ease up on the food-related penances until I had a few more years of mental and physical health under my belt (which I strongly advise other people in the process of recovering from an eating disorder to do).

As my eating disorder slipped more and more into the past, however, entering into the Church's cycle of fasting and feasting became an important part of the final stages of my recovery. To a certain extent, that's because fasting kept my newfound attachment to food in check, ensuring that Christ, not my stomach, always came first.

The real benefit, though, came not so much from the fasting as from the feasting.

Pan Fried Gnocchi Aglio e Olio

Serves: 4

You can eat nothing but bread on days of fasting and abstinence. Or you can eat this simple, tasty meal that's a staple in my kitchen on Fridays during Lent (and throughout the year).

Ingredients

24 ounces boxed (or home-
made) potato gnocchi

2 tablespoons olive oil

2 tablespoons butter

2 cloves garlic, smashed

1 tablespoon crushed red
pepper flakes (optional)

¼ cup chopped parsley

¼ cup chopped basil

½ cup Pecorino-Romano
(or Parmesan) cheese,
freshly shredded

Kosher salt

Bring 6 cups of water to boil. When water is a few minutes from reaching its boiling point, combine olive oil and butter in a large frying pan and melt together over medium heat. Add crushed garlic to butter and oil, and toast until it reaches a golden brown. Remove garlic from oil and set aside.

When water starts to boil, add gnocchi. Boil until the gnocchi floats to the surface (about 3–4 minutes). Using a slotted spoon, remove gnocchi from the boiling water and transfer to the frying pan. Toss the gnocchi in butter and oil, and cook until they become lightly brown and slightly crisp. Toss in herbs and crushed red pepper flakes. Divide evenly onto plates and sprinkle with Pecorino-Romano. Check for salt.

CHAPTER EIGHT

Holy Feast
Rejoicing with Christ

Years ago, while perusing a dusty old junk shop with a friend, I happened across a tarnished silver serving tray. It wasn't solid silver—just silver plate—but it was beautiful. It was also five dollars. I bought it on the spot.

When I returned home I found some silver polish, cleaned up the platter, and used it to serve hors d'oeuvres at my next dinner party. I felt like the poshest hostess on the block. Considering that, at the time, I lived in a Washington, DC ghetto, that wasn't much of a stretch.

After I moved to Steubenville and took up residence in another ghetto, I discovered that the antique stores in the area were full up with cheap silver plate, leftovers from the city's more prosperous days. Thus my obsession began in earnest.

As a poor graduate student and fledgling writer, I wasn't always flush with cash, but Steubenville silver was a luxury I could afford. Bit by bit, year by year, my little collection grew, until it reached the point where I owned enough silver to set a spread fit for royalty—dozens of platters and bowls; multiple coffee pots, tea pots, creamers and sugars; two sets of flatware, and all sorts of charming miniature plates perfect for cookies, nuts, and other treats.

At my wedding, we carted boxes of the stuff to the reception venue, using it to decorate mantles and tabletops. It looked lovely. Most of the time, though, my silver collection gets put to use for much humbler affairs: Easter brunches, Thanksgiving dinners, Christmas parties, and the countless little parties my friends and I throw to celebrate the Church's liturgical feasts.

To some, whipping out a silver serving platter every Ascension Thursday might seem like overkill. But for me, those feasts aren't just occasions to show off my flea market finds. They're opportunities to help the people I love experience a small foretaste of the glorious feast God calls us to in eternity. Silver serving pieces, in their way, hint at the riches that await us there.

So too does the food they hold.

Depending on the day or the season, those silver platters are laden with bacon-wrapped dates, pepper-laced beef tenderloin, and honey-soaked ham. Peppermint meltaways, my grandmother's cashew chocolate clusters, and lemon-cheesecake bars also know those platters well. Roasted vegetables of every sort, mashed potatoes whipped together with heavy cream, butter, and garlic, and salads bursting with dried fruits and nuts have all filled my silver bowls. Whether I'm serving five people or seventy-five, feast days at my house mean the table is set with a beautiful, shining abundance.

Which is just as it should be.

"Good talk and good food go naturally together."

LEON KASS, *THE HUNGRY SOUL: EATING AND THE PERFECTING OF OUR NATURE*

FEASTING FOR A CAUSE

If you're searching the Church calendar for the greatest feasts and greatest fasts, you'll usually find them cozied up next to each other, with the fasts preparing us for the feasts to come, and the feasts helping us better understand the fasts just passed (see CCC 2043). In the balance, though, Christians who plan their meals according to the liturgical calendar will find themselves doing a great deal more feasting than fasting.

In the Catholic Church, every season of fasting is followed by a longer season of feasting. Lent is forty days. Easter is fifty. Advent lasts a little over four weeks. Christmas lasts a solid five and half weeks, beginning on December 25 and running right up to February 2, the Feast of the Presentation.

Moreover, while the Latin Church mandates two days of fasting (Ash Wednesday and Good Friday) plus another forty-eight or so days of abstinence (most other Fridays throughout the year), her calendar provides about three times as many opportunities for feasting.

We feast on Christmas Day and Easter Day, Holy Days of Obligation, Solemnities, and every single Sunday, all of which the Church considers "little Easters." We also can choose to celebrate favorite saints and martyrs on the dozens and dozens of days set aside to remember them. Heck, we can even feast in honor of buildings. The papal basilica of St. John Lateran and the Portiuncula chapel rebuilt by St. Francis both have feasts of their own (November 9 and August 2, respectively).

In the Catholic Church, we always have cause for feasting. Which is grand for someone who likes hosting parties as much as I do. But the ultimate cause for our feasting is never a saint or a stunning work of architecture. The ultimate cause is always Christ.

"Feasting is a collective celebration of God's presence among us given as bread. Feasting is a collective expression of gratitude for this superabundant divine edible gift. But it is also a call to incorporate (by sharing with one another) the whole community into this expression of thanksgiving."

ANGEL F. MENDEZ-MONTOYA, *THE THEOLOGY OF FOOD: EATING AND THE EUCHARIST*

A SHORT HISTORY OF FEASTING

Feasting, like fasting, is an eminently human activity. The Greeks, the Romans, the blue-painted Picts, and just about every other grouping of men and women since Adam and Eve have set aside days for indulging in the best that creation has to offer.

Many of those feasts have been religious in nature; people feasted to honor the gods (or God) in which they believed. Other feasts were celebratory; they commemorated victories in battle, triumphs over disease, or the survival of particularly harsh winters. And even more feasts took place simply for the host to impress his friends, enemies, and neighbors. Some feasts were thrown for a combination of all three reasons.

Depending on the location, the host, and the people being served, the nature of those feasts have varied. Many feasts have been relatively tame affairs. For example, the Kwakiutl people of British Columbia marked their annual gift-giving feast, Potlatch, with strips of seal blubber and crabapples, both soused in fish oil. Not exactly foodie fare, but festive in its context.[1]

---

[1] Nichola Fletcher, "A Short History of Pigging Out," *Forbes*, November 15, 2007, http://www.forbes.com/2007/11/11/feasts-history-parties-forbeslife-food07-cx_nf_1115feasts.html.

Other feasts have been madly extravagant. In the first century AD, the Roman Emperor Vitellius served his guests peacock brains and flamingo tongues. Two centuries later, one of his successors, Heliogabalus, laced his guests' food with precious gemstones and nuggets of gold.[2]

The dietary restrictions of Leviticus meant flamingo tongues were never on the menu for the ancient Israelites, but Abraham's descendants still got in on the feasting game. They feasted to welcome strangers, celebrate betrothals and marriages, rejoice after triumphs in battle, and even to mark the weaning of a child (Gen 18:4–8; 29:21–22; Judg 14:10; 1 Macc 4:36; Gen 21:8).

More importantly, three times a year the Israelites feasted at God's command, celebrating the Feast of Passover, the Feast of Weeks, and the Feast of Tabernacles (Ex 23:14–16). Each feast commemorated some great deed God had done for them in the past (rescuing their ancestors from slavery, giving the law, and delivering Israel from their wilderness wanderings). The feasts also anticipated Israel's future deliverance through the promised Messiah.

Jesus, being the good Jew that he was, followed the traditions of his ancestors and partook in the feasts of his people. He celebrated Passover with his disciples. He dined for seven days at the wedding in Cana (a feast which makes even today's most Pinterest-inspired weddings look tame). And he sat at table with tax collectors, prostitutes, and wine bibbers, eating and talking with them.

So much feasting went on in Jesus' presence that John's disciples protested. Why did John fast on locusts and honey, while the disciples of Jesus feasted?

Jesus answered: "Can you make wedding guests fast while the bridegroom is with them? The days will come, when the

---

[2] Ibid.

bridegroom is taken away from them, and then they will fast in those days" (Lk 5:34–35).

<hr/>

GLUTTONY

Feasting—merrily, moderately, and liturgically—is a good thing. Gluttony, however, is not. Classified by the Church as one of the seven deadly sins, gluttony is a vicious form of self-love that puts the body's natural appetites above kindness, charity, consideration for others, and the moral imperative to provide for the poor.

Contrary to popular opinion, when the Church preaches against gluttony, she's not simply preaching against over-eating. The sin of gluttony entails much more than eating too much. As St. Gregory the Great and St. Thomas Aquinas explained, we are guilty of gluttony when we eat "hastily, sumptuously, too much, greedily, daintily."[3]

Spelled out in more detail, that means we commit the sin of gluttony when we eat just to eat and not because we're hungry (hastily); when we regularly or exclusively dine on only the most expensive and richest foods (sumptuously); when we overeat (too much); when we take more than our fair share of food (greedily); and when we insist upon eating only certain foods or refuse foods that are not grown, prepared, or served in very specific ways (daintily).

So . . . the bowl of ice cream you had before dinner, when you weren't even hungry? Gluttony.

Your insistence on shopping for pantry staples at Dean and Deluca? Gluttony.

That second helping of cheesecake you had last night? Gluttony.

<hr/>

[3] Aquinas, *Summa*, II-II, q. 148, a.4.

Dishing up for yourself an extra-large portion of stew before everyone else at the dinner table got served? Gluttony.

Refusing to eat the baked fish your mom worked hard to prepare because you only like your fish fried? Gluttony.

Demanding that the friend hosting you for a weekend plan all the meals around your current "clean eating" fast? Gluttony.

So, how do we avoid being gluttons?

First, we pray. Because without God's grace, avoiding gluttony in this day and age is no easy task. Second, since gluttony is rooted in self-love, we counter it by growing in humility. We deny ourselves what we don't need, choose simple fare for our daily meals, moderate our portions, give others the bigger piece of pie, serve ourselves last, and eat whatever is served to us. Even beets.

No one said being a saint would be easy.

The Marriage Supper of the Lamb

Jesus' disciples did fast after he ascended to heaven. The Book of Acts and other early records of the Apostles' ministry, such as the *Didache*, attest to that. But his disciples also feasted, gathering together on Sundays for the Eucharist and for a common meal (often referred to as the *agape* meal or "love feast"). The first Christians did these things not in contradiction to Jesus' words in Luke 5:34–35, but rather in obedience to them.

Christ, after all, is the Bridegroom. His people, the Church, are the Bride. Union with him is our hope and goal. It's our destiny . . . if we don't forsake it for sin.

That destiny is described by Isaiah as a banquet, where God will "make for all peoples a feast of fat things, a feast of choice

wines—of fat things full of marrow, of choice wines well refined"
(Is 25:6).

The Psalmist also speaks of God's children feasting "on the
abundance of [his] house" and drinking "from the river of [his]
delights" (Ps 36:8), while Jesus himself compares the kingdom of
heaven to "a marriage feast" thrown by a king for his son (Mt 22:2).

Later, the Book of Revelation tells us that the end of salvation history is a wedding banquet. The angels issue a call—"Come,
gather for the great supper of God" (Rev 19:17). They also promise blessing to all who answer the call—"Blessed are those who are
invited to the marriage supper of the Lamb" (19:9).

This is how God wants us to see heaven: as the people of God,
feasting without restraint on his presence, drinking in the Trinity's
beauty, goodness, truth, and love to the point of holy intoxication.

"Let [the Bride of Christ] drink as much as she desires and get
drunk on all these wines in the cellar of God!" wrote St. Teresa
of Avila, meditating on that holy feast. "Let her enjoy these joys,
wonder at these great things, and not fear to lose her life through
drinking much more than her weak nature enables her to do. Let
her die at last in this paradise of delights; blessed death that makes
one live in such a way."[4]

Fasting teaches us about our hunger, our dependency, our
need for Christ. Feasting, understood in the light of faith, teaches
us about answered prayers, about a God who fills our emptiness
and satisfies our hunger beyond our greatest imaginings. It foreshadows the great feast yet to come, whetting the appetite of all
who partake in it for the marriage supper of the Lamb.

That's why Christ's first followers feasted. They feasted in an-
ticipation of that ultimate feast. And that's why Christians continue
to feast.

---

[4]   Christopher West, *Fill These Hearts: God, Sex, and Human Longing* (New
York: Random House, 2013), 38.

No matter how grand or humble, every Christian feast is a foreshadowing—or more accurately, a foretaste—of the heavenly wedding feast. For even though we can't look on Christ face to face just yet, he is with us. He is present in his Church. He is present in the Eucharist. And where he is present, we feast.

PATRON SAINTS OF COOKING:
ST. DROGO

For centuries, coffee bean growers, roasters, and shopkeepers have relied upon St. Drogo for help with their work, even though the twelfth-century Flemish nobleman turned shepherd (then pilgrim . . . then hermit) had no known connection with coffee. Rather, legend has it that he survived mostly on bread and warm water.

Legend also tells us, however, that St. Drogo had the gift of bilocation. Local villagers regularly reported his simultaneous presence both in the fields and at Mass. So, perhaps the saint's ability to fit more into his day than was humanly possible explains his connection to the over-caffeinated set.

PRACTICE MAKES PERFECT

The first Christians feasted every Sunday, which they recognized as a "little Easter," a memorial of Christ's Resurrection. On that day, they did as Christ commanded: they remembered him in the breaking of bread and the blessing of wine. In that remembering, Jesus came again, glorified and transfigured, the Bridegroom with his Bride once more. His coming was understood as an occasion for feasting, both on the Eucharist and on ordinary food (the *agape* feast mentioned earlier), in which the early Christians partook either before or after the Eucharistic breaking of the bread.[5]

Over time, the Church separated the celebration of the Eucharist and the *agape* feast. People came together for the Eucharist, then they went to their own homes for a meal.[6] Sundays, however, remained "little Easters," and even the strictest ascetics broke their penitential fasts to enjoy Sunday supper.

Before long, Christians began commemorating other special holy days, such as Easter and Christmas, in a similar manner: liturgically, with a Mass, and privately, with a special meal. The two meals—the Lord's Supper and the family's supper—were of a piece. The higher and holier the liturgical feast, the grander and more elaborate the meal.

As the centuries passed, the family and community celebrations that took place on days of liturgical feasting became as filled with tradition as the liturgies they accompanied. There were songs and games and prayers that went along with the day, and most important there were special foods unique to the occasion, all of which helped Christians enter into the spirit of the holidays (literally "holy days") with greater gusto.

Today, many of those food traditions live on.

On Christmas Eve, the Italians prepare for the coming Christ Child with the Feast of Seven Fishes. The Irish do the same with Oyster Stew. Christmas Day means turkeys and plum pudding

---

[5]   Darrel J. Pursiful, "The Earliest Liturgy Developments," Dr. Platypus (blog), March 24, 2008, https://pursiful.com/2008/03/22/the-earliest-liturgy-developments/; Darrel J. Pursiful, "Why Did Eucharist and Agape Diverge," Dr. Platypus (blog), March 24, 2008, https://pursiful.com/2008/03/24/why-did-eucharist-and-agape-diverge/.

[6]   Some scholars blame the persecution of the Church and the need for shorter, earlier gatherings. Another camp points to Paul's First Letter to the Corinthians, which hints at a lack of Christian charity and decorum during the meal.

for the English, while Easter brings roasts of lamb and ham. On Pentecost Sunday, families across Europe cook doves, Cornish rock hens, and other small birds, tipping their culinary hats to the Third Person of the Holy Trinity, often depicted as a holy bird. They also make a fruit salad with twelve different types of fruit, each one symbolizing a fruit of the Holy Spirit.

Saints eventually got their own specialty dishes as well. In Northern France, on St. Catherine of Alexandria's feast day, Catholics bake heart-shaped cakes, called St. Catherine's cakes, and give them to young unmarried women who hope for a husband. In Italy, St. Martin of Tours is celebrated with his own coffeecake. Other saintly culinary treats include St. Sylvester's Punch, St. Joseph's Rice Fritters, and St. Lucy's Crown Bread.

COOKING WITH CATHOLICS

Wondering what to cook on All Saints Day? Not sure what cocktail to mix on St. Thomas Aquinas' feast day? These Catholic-flavored cookbooks can help.

- *Cooking with the Saints* by Ernst Schuegraf
- *Drinking with the Saints* by Michael P. Foley
- *The Catholic Home: Celebrations and Traditions for Holidays, Feast Days and Every Day* by Meredith Gould
- *Grace Before Meals: Recipes and Inspiration for Family Meals and Family Life* by Fr. Leo Patalinghug
- *A Continual Feast: A Cookbook to Celebrate the Joys of Family and Faith Throughout the Christian Year* by Evelyn Birge Vitz

All the Trimmings

Cooking these special dishes was and is work. Cooking for any holiday is work. Just ask any host who prepares Christmas dinner. All good feasts worth their salt require hours, if not days, in the kitchen peeling, chopping, stirring, roasting. They also require weeks of planning, shopping, cleaning, setting the table, and decking the halls. If that's true today (and trust me, it is), when fancy gas ovens, KitchenAid mixers, and Breville food processors do half the work for us, imagine what Easter breakfast required in a world without electricity!

Nevertheless, despite all that feasting requires, Christian women and men still have logged countless hours in the kitchen, year after year, preparing feast after feast. And many—or at least some—have logged those hours without complaint. Quite a few even have logged the hours with joy. Their work has been made lighter by the reason behind it: the Bridegroom is coming.

On Easter, on Christmas, on every Sunday of the year, that's what we celebrate. We celebrate him. We celebrate *with* him. We feast with Jesus Christ and all of heaven, rejoicing in God's life, God's love, and God's great gift of himself to us.

And yes, we celebrate those truths in church. We celebrate them with liturgy and song and smoky incense that rises up to heaven like a prayer. But that's not enough. It's never been enough for a sacramental people.

Every day, on every altar, the Bridegroom becomes heavenly food for us. As such, making our joy in his love and life incarnate through earthly food is the most natural thing in the world. To pour our time, our energy, our creativity, and our money into preparing special foods on special feasts is simply to imitate him who provides us with the most special feast of all.

Moreover, because he gave us his best, on feast days we give him our best—not Queen Elizabeth's best, but the best our humble selves can manage. For one person, that might mean a five-course meal for twenty. For someone else, that might mean stirring a bit of meat into a simple soup or stew. For most Catholics, it's almost always meant pouring wine, beer, or some special drink that stirs the soul to merriment. And it's also almost always meant doing something good with sugar. Because what's a feast day without dessert?

It's not just the food that makes a feast special, though. It's also how we serve it. It's me whipping out my silver. It's you leaving the paper plates in the cupboard and eating off Grandma's china instead. It's lighting candles, using real napkins, real glassware, and sitting everyone down around the dining room table, cleared (for the occasion) of homework, papers, and bills. It's taking five extra minutes, if that's all we can spare, to try to make manifest at our tables the beauty and wonder of the mystery we're celebrating. On feast days, the Church outfits the altars and her priests with special cloths, vestments, and floral arrangements. We just follow her lead when we outfit the domestic church with the best our china cabinets and linen closets have to offer.

More important than any fancy foods or fancy dishes, however, are the people doing the feasting. While minor feast days don't require a crowd (an extra piece of chocolate after lunch will suffice), the major feasts do. The marriage supper of the Lamb is not supper for one, and Christmas Dinner isn't meant to be eaten alone. Both are meals to share with friends, neighbors, extended family members, and lonely souls in need of a dinner invitation. The Communion of Saints feasting in heaven is a dinner crowd without number. Welcoming others to feast with us images that heavenly feast. It enlivens it and enriches it with laughter, conversation, and friendship. In that it reminds us that ultimately, we're called to more than a feast: we're called to communion.

* * *

And that brings us back to my story.

In the early years of my recovery, I made feasting a matter of obedience. If the Church said, "Feast," I feasted like it was my job. During Christmas and Easter, as well as on holy days of obligation and solemnities, I treated the Church's designated feast days as a personal order from on High to eat cookies and drink an extra glass of wine. I also started cooking special meals for friends on the bigger feast days. For me, those days became an excuse to throw a party and be with the people I loved . . . as well as to use my silver.

Basically, I entered into the spirit of feasting with gusto, making my joy in Christ and his saints incarnate in what I served for dinner. In that feasting, I eventually found the freedom to fast with the Church as well.

With time, I could give up sweets during Lent and not feel like I was restricting myself or proving how disciplined I could be. It wasn't about me at all anymore. I was just eating with the Church in preparation for Easter. Likewise, when Easter arrived, I could eat chocolate every day without guilt. Jesus said feast. I was just following instructions.

In a sense, I surrendered my desire to restrict and indulge to Christ. I submitted my appetites, both for control and for food, to his Church. In her natural rhythms of feasting and fasting, I found a happy peace, born of solidarity with Christ.

I also found something I wasn't expecting, but probably should have: a better me.

CHOCOLATE CASHEW CLUSTERS

Makes approximately 100 clusters

When I was a little girl, I lived for my grandma's chocolate pea-nut clusters. Then, in my early twenties, I went and developed a peanut allergy. Now, I only live if I *don't* eat my grandma's pea-nut clusters. One bite, and no more breathing for me. Fortunately, cashews and I get along just fine—so fine actually, that even if peanuts didn't make my throat close up, I'd still prefer this adapta-tion of my childhood favorite.

Ingredients

2 pounds white candy/baking bark

18 ounces semi-sweet chocolate chips

2 squares dark baking chocolate

3 pounds cashews

wax paper

Spread out wax paper on your countertop . . . and table . . . and any other flat surface you can find. This recipe makes a ton of candy.

Once you've papered your kitchen with wax, take a large, heavy-bottomed pot and melt all the chocolate over low (low!) heat, stirring continuously. When it is completely melted, add cashews and combine well. Drop by the spoonful onto wax paper. Allow to cool and harden. Store in an airtight container in the refrigerator for up to a month.

CHAPTER NINE

Table Lessons
Eating and the Virtues

T he Church's call to feast and the Church's command to fast are, at least in my world, two of her greatest gifts. When done rightly and done well, feasting and fasting bring the whole person—body and soul—into the liturgical rhythms of the Church. They make the liturgical seasons incarnate in our homes and communities. They also help form communities, uniting rich and poor, young and old, married and single in a common practice: eating . . . or not eating as the case may be.

From the first months of my return to the Catholic faith I recognized this. It didn't require a great deal of thinking or work on my part to see the value of feasting and fasting. But what did require thinking and work was doing it right.

I am a creature of extremes. I blame it on my red hair. My tendency, like many a ginger, is all or nothing. Balance, moderation, temperance—they don't come naturally to me. My approach to fasting and feasting was no exception. Remember the Lent of the crashing, burning, vegan, Mormon celiac? That's pure Emily.

Feasting was trickier still. There were just so many Feast Days. Was I supposed to eat cheesecake on all of them? If so, how much cheesecake? Was the Church cool with two pieces? What about three? Four definitely seemed like too much, but where did feasting end and gluttony begin? How did one draw the line?

I had similar queries about all the days in between the fasting and feasting— what the Church calls Ordinary Time. How, without my strict diet to guide me, was I supposed to navigate all the choices presented to me by our consumer culture? I wanted to appreciate the abundance of creation. I wanted to nourish my body and soul with God's great gift of food. I just wasn't sure how to find the right balance.

I didn't find the solution to that dilemma overnight. There were no bolt-from-the-blue revelations in churches or bookstores. I just plowed ahead, sometimes eating too much, sometimes eating too little, but always trying to approach feasting, fasting, and ordinary eating with an eye to what God wanted from me in that particular moment. And slowly, gradually, I came to see that my trying *was* what God wanted from me. Eating itself offered me the opportunity to learn balance.

For years, I'd thought of eating as an opportunity for vice—for gluttony or greed. But what I failed to grasp is that eating is also an opportunity for virtue. It's a daily invitation to flex our spiritual muscles and grow in justice, prudence, temperance, and fortitude. It's also a chance to demonstrate faith, hope, and charity.

GOING TO EXTREMES

Our consumer culture doesn't see eating this way. It wants to encourage the inner redhead in all of us and tempt us to extremes. Social media testifies to this in spades.

For example, come December, my various newsfeeds are glutted with pictures of savory sides and tasty treats. Recipes for peppermint shortbread cookies, hot buttered rum, and sausage-cranberry meatballs abound. Then, in January, it's all "Whole 30 this" and "Paleo that." The same phenomenon happens at Easter. One day, people are waxing rhapsodic about coconut raspberry scones; the next, everyone is condemning gluten like it's the second coming of the Black Death.

Note: some people have legitimate problems with certain foods. I'm one of them. Peanuts make me stop breathing. It's exceptionally annoying and often inconvenient. Food allergies and serious sensitivities always have my sympathy. But a good many of the people in my newsfeed who post close-ups of chocolate almond puff pastry one day and sing the praises of eating like cavemen the next struggle more with temperance than they do with dietary sensitivities.

I get the struggle. It's mine too. We live in a culture of abundance, where bottomless baskets of breadsticks welcome us in every restaurant, 468 different kinds of breakfast cereal line the supermarket shelves, and thousands of food blogs tempt us daily with tasty treats.

That abundance has made some of us sick. It has made others among us a bit rounder than we'd like to be. Accordingly, the appeal of extreme diets, which promise good health and slim waistlines in exchange for eliminating whole categories of food, is understandable. Sometimes, the way of total abstinence just seems easier . . . and safer.

Which it may be. But it's also rarely sustainable. Or enjoyable. That's why diets almost always fail and why my Whole 30-loving friends are back to making cupcakes the day after their thirty days of "clean eating" end. Most of us don't want to live in a world without donuts or pizza or dirty martinis. Nor, every time we eat outside our houses, do we want to be a total pain in the rear, demanding special treatment from friends hosting us for dinner or restaurants cooking us dinner.

This is why exercising virtue when we eat matters so much.

"The most efficacious means of keeping in mind the rules of temperance, and obtaining strength to follow them, is to say, piously, the prayer before and after meals. By this we shall draw down upon ourselves the blessing of God, and obtain the grace not to offend Him."

ST. JEAN-BAPTISTE DE LA SALLE

HABIT FORMING

Before we go any further, let's review our Catechism.

Virtue, it tells us, is a "habitual and firm disposition to do the good" (CCC 1833). More simply, it's a habit of doing the right thing—of acting honest, brave, kind, generous, and all sorts of other good things.

From there, the Catechism breaks down virtue into two basic categories: human virtues and theological virtues.

Human virtues are good habits we acquire primarily through our own efforts. A variety of virtues fall into this category (chastity, modesty, honesty, etc.), but the Church generally recognizes four virtues as "cardinal," meaning they make practicing the other human virtues possible. These are: prudence (knowing the good), justice (doing the good we ought to do), fortitude (doing the good even when it's difficult), and temperance (balancing competing goods in service of the ultimate good).

Our ability to exercise these cardinal virtues depends on three things: temperament, grace, and work.

First, there's temperament, meaning different human virtues come more easily to some people than they do to others. Much depends on our natural gifts and personalities. For me, fortitude is easy; temperance not so much. Again . . . the hair.

Grace is even more foundational. God's grace makes every good action of ours possible. Even the virtues to which we're more innately inclined are a gift of grace. Without God's grace, I couldn't manage to exercise the least bit of fortitude, no matter how hard I tried.

Nevertheless, even taking God's grace and our natural inclinations into account, our ability to exercise the human virtues hinges largely on our own efforts. And those efforts require time. Prudence, temperance, fortitude, and justice aren't perfected overnight. Like in sports, cooking, painting, or just about any other skill, so too with the virtues: practice makes perfect. Most of us have to do the moral and spiritual equivalent of soccer drills, practicing the virtues over and over again, to reach the point where the virtues come naturally and easily.

Again, that's not to say we don't need God's grace to act virtuously. Every human being on this planet needs God's grace to do anything good. But believers and unbelievers alike are capable of practicing the human virtues. Faith in Christ isn't a prerequisite for being just. It just makes being just easier.

Once we've made a habit of doing good, however, all of life becomes, in a sense, easier. We have an easier time knowing the good and doing the good. We have an easier time being who God made us to be and living how God made us to live. By freeing us from the pull of vicious habits, the virtues make us more fully human. They help us live richer human lives.

That brings us to the second category of virtues: the theological virtues of faith, hope, and charity.

While the human virtues free us up to live a more fully human life, the theological virtues dispose us to live a divine life. More specifically, faith helps us believe in God and all he has revealed. Hope helps us desire heaven. And charity helps us love God and neighbor. Together, all three theological virtues till the soil of our souls, so that God's grace can bear more fruit in us and so that we can enter more deeply into a relationship with him. The theological virtues also help us pursue the human virtues with greater grace, making it easier for our fallen selves to live loving lives.

Unlike the human virtues, though, we don't need to work to acquire the theological virtues. We actually can't work to acquire them. God infuses these virtues straight into our souls. They are pure gift. We can pray for greater faith, hope, and charity. We can do things to better dispose ourselves to receive them—like putting ourselves in front of the Blessed Sacrament more frequently. But we can't merit the theological virtues. When it comes to growing in faith, hope, and charity, God does all the heavy lifting.

"If more of us valued food and cheer and song above hoarded gold it would be a merrier world."

J. R. R. TOLKIEN, *THE HOBBIT*

TABLE LESSONS

Everyday God presents us with opportunities to grow in the human virtues.

When we're late for work in the morning, we can weave perilously in and out of traffic, cutting off other cars in our quest to beat the clock, or we can follow the rules of the road. That is, we can choose to act justly (and in the process become a more just person) or we can choose to act unjustly (and become a more unjust person).

Likewise, when the clock strikes 10 p.m. and we remember we have an early breakfast meeting the next day, we can choose to shut off the television and get ready for bed . . . or we can continue binge watching *Breaking Bad* on Netflix until 3 a.m. So, we can exercise prudence (and grow in prudence) or we can fail to exercise prudence . . . and miss our breakfast meeting.

One of the most consistent opportunities most of us have to practice our human virtues and exercise the theological virtues, however, comes at mealtime.

Every day, each of us must repeatedly decide if we will eat with justice, prudence, fortitude, and temperance. In the face of our appetites, our emotional needs, personal preferences, and an abundance of food, each of us has to choose the good for our body and soul, and then do the good for our body and soul.

Strength Training

Let's break that down, starting with justice.

Justice is the first and most foundational virtue for healthy, happy, balanced eating. A just man wants to give God and his neighbor "their due" (CCC 1807). He wants to treat both God and man as they should be treated. He also wants to treat himself justly. He wants to give himself his due.

In the realm of eating, justice helps us want to eat right. It is the habitual exercise of the will that makes us prefer vegetables over Twinkies, water over soda, and salmon over Spam. It also makes us want to eat the right amount of food and not be wasteful, so that we don't gorge ourselves while others starve. Lastly, it helps us want to give God his due by obeying his command to fast on fast days and to feast on feast days. In essence, justice helps us will the good for our body and soul.

Prudence is the virtue that guides our thinking as we pursue that good. It enables us to "discern our true good in every circumstance" (CCC 1806). So, it's prudence that helps us recognize that an apple is a better snack than a Hot Pocket. It's prudence that helps us understand that we should eat a little more than normal when we're pregnant or nursing. And it's prudence that dictates we eat broccoli, not just a plate of plain pasta, at dinnertime because we really do need to eat our vegetables.

Prudence also can show us that it's unwise to eat when we're bored and wise to eat before we take a test. It can help us recognize the good of treating ourselves to a celebratory meal when we get a promotion at work and the bad of eating a pint of Ben and Jerry's when our boyfriend dumps us. In what we eat and don't eat, prudence enables us to make wise, healthy choices.

Fortitude is what helps us make those wise, healthy choices not just on one day, but every day. It's the virtue that "ensures firmness in difficulties and constancy in the pursuit of the good"; it also "strengthens the resolve to resist temptations" (CCC 1808).

So, fortitude helps us choose the apple, not the Hot Pocket, for our snack on Monday and then again on Tuesday, Wednesday, Thursday, and Friday. It helps us drink eight glasses of water and eat several servings of vegetables daily, not just once in a while. And, as a matter of routine, it helps us walk past the cookies, coffeecakes, and other tasty treats our co-workers bring into the office. Essentially, fortitude is the virtue that makes our commitment to healthy, balanced eating more than a flash in the pan. It makes it a way of life.

Last but not least, temperance helps coordinate all those other virtues and enables us to practice moderation in all things. As the Catechism explains, temperance "moderates the attraction of pleasures and provides balance in the use of created goods" (1809).

It's temperance that tells us it's okay to have one cookie after lunch, but not four; one piece of cheesecake on a feast day, not two; one dirty martini at night, and no more. It's also temperance that tells us that a Lenten fast of bread and water is not a good idea for a body not used to fasting or for a busy mom who needs to take care of her family. It's temperance that helps us choose a salad for lunch if we plan to indulge in a rich smorgasbord of appetizers a few hours later at the office Christmas party. And it's temperance that tells us it's good to avoid fast food and preservatives, but that an occasional run through McDonalds isn't going to kill us.

Basically, temperance makes us sane. It prevents us from going to extremes, and enables us to enjoy all the good food and drink in creation without falling into the sin of gluttony.

The Family Meal

Looking for a surefire way to become a more virtuous eater? All you have to do is start eating more regularly in your home with friends and family.

Eating with others teaches us patience: we have to wait for others to be served before serving ourselves. It also teaches us temperance: we have to make sure everyone has enough to eat. It teaches us prudence: we learn how to make good choices by watching others make good choices. It teaches us humility: we sometimes have to eat things we would not choose to eat if we were cooking for (or only for) ourselves. And it teaches us justice: we have to moderate expensive purchases when regularly feeding a crowd.

Through it all, at the family dinner table we learn to put people ahead of food. It can become, essentially, a school for charity, helping us to grow in understanding and love over a really good meal.

118   EMILY STIMPSON CHAPMAN

The theological virtues come into play a little differently. Faith, hope, and charity don't necessarily dictate how we eat, but they do shape how we think about eating and approach cooking for and eating with others.

Faith, for example, reminds us that eating isn't just about nourishing our bodies; it's also about nourishing our souls and growing in virtue. Likewise, faith reminds us to give thanks for what's before us; it helps us see all the food on our table and in our cupboards as a sign of God's provision. In that, it also asks us to trust that God will provide for us tomorrow, much as he provided for us today. It was a lack of faith that led the Israelites to hoard manna and quail in the wilderness (Ex 16), and a similar lack of faith can lead us to hoard our own food and not share it with others.

Hope keeps our eyes on Christ as we eat. It checks our tendency to prioritize the earthly over the heavenly, and reminds us that there are more important things in life than our bellies. Hope also helps us to not despair when we fail to eat with justice, prudence, fortitude, or temperance. It reminds us that tomorrow is another day, with new graces awaiting us and new opportunities to accept those graces. Lastly, hope helps us see all our failures (and successes) in light of Christ's promise that his grace is sufficient. In that, it enables us to rely on his strength, not our own, as we face temptation and prepare to do battle with our appetites and all the emotions and fears that might lead us to abuse the gift of food.

And charity? Charity helps us think of others before ourselves. At the most basic level, it asks us to feed the poor by contributing money, time, or food to those who don't have enough. It also helps us, when possible, choose food that is grown or manufactured in an ethical way, without hurting people or creation.

On a deeper, more fundamental level, charity helps us to think of others in how we cook, eat, and shop. So, it helps us set aside our personal dislike of spaghetti so we can make it for our husband, who loves noodles and marinara sauce beyond all reason. When there's only one piece of apple pie left on the table, charity helps us take a pass on indulging our own cravings and instead offer the piece to a guest. Charity also helps us hold our tongue when a friend serves us dried-out chicken and politely eat what they've generously prepared for us. It calls us to overcome pickiness, which St. Thomas and Gregory the Great both categorized as a form of gluttony, asking us to set aside our personal dietary preferences when we eat in others' homes and appreciate the gifts they're giving to us through their cooking.

Or, to sum it all up, charity is what keeps us from being the annoying, rude, and selfish guest whom no one likes to serve.

Cross Training

Every time we choose to abstain from meat on Friday and put a little extra money in the poor box instead, we grow in justice. Every time we opt for water over soda, we grow a little bit more prudent. Every time we stick to our commitment to eat a nutritious salad for lunch our fortitude increases. And every time we eat just one cookie and leave the rest for later, we become more temperate. The choices we make every day about food move us closer to (or farther away from) the virtuous life.

Our ability to make those choices, however, increases when we make them outside the kitchen as well. Some of us . . . okay, most of us . . . really struggle to say no to the second cookie. The pull of tasty treats is strong, and while we may desire to exercise our virtues at table, that desire often loses out in the face of other desires—like the desire to eat more bacon.

This is where spiritual cross training comes in. For almost two millennia, holy men and women have advised that the best way to overcome a vice is by practicing the opposite virtue. For example, they explained, if your pride repeatedly leads you to lose your temper, than you need to look for opportunities to practice humility: take the worst seat in the room, don't correct someone when they're wrong, let someone else win the argument.

In a similar way, this approach works with eating and the virtues. If temperance always fails you in the kitchen, look for opportunities to practice it elsewhere: buy only one new pair of shoes instead of two; watch only one episode of *Buffy the Vampire Slayer*, not three; look at Facebook for five minutes, not fifty. Alternately, if eating with fortitude is your downfall, try to master the virtue in other areas of your life: pick a bedtime and stick to it, commit to an exercise routine and honor that commitment, do the hardest task at work first thing every day.

The same theory applies to growing in justice: use your turn signal every time you change lanes, don't fudge on your taxes, speak up when the restaurant leaves an item off your bill. As for prudence, think three times before you post a snarky comment on Twitter; don't buy the new sweater you like right away—take twenty-four hours to think about it; and before you make a big financial or professional decision, seek out the advice of someone wiser than yourself.

In all those ways and more, we can strengthen our spiritual muscles and grow in virtue, which will come in handy both in and out of the kitchen.

As for faith, hope, and charity? Well, we can't master those. They're gifts. But we can work at thinking about food and eating through a prism of faith, hope, and charity. We can look at our own habits and assess where we might be failing to apply our theology to our practices in the kitchen. We also can pray. We can put ourselves in front of the Eucharist, confess our sins, and ask God for greater grace. He likes it when we do that, and he always delivers.

THE CATHOLIC TABLE   121

Not maybe in the way we expect or in the time frame we give him, but God never says no to requests for greater faith, hope, and charity (Mt 7:9–11). And in the long run, the more faith, hope, and charity we have, the more we can relax and enjoy our nightly supper.

BEYOND VIRTUE

Every meal offers us the opportunity to grow in virtue. But is every occasion where we fail to eat prudently, temperately, justly, or with fortitude a failure of virtue? In other words, is every person who pigged out on pizza or pie last night guilty of intemperance or imprudence? Was their pigging out their fault? A free choice for which they bear the blame?

Not necessarily.

On one level, eating six pieces of pizza or an entire cherry pie is almost always an intemperate and imprudent action. But different circumstances can mitigate our responsibility for such actions. People who have habitually used food to deal with emotional and spiritual struggles—who eat to cope with their fear, anxiety, grief, stress, or frustration—can't just flip a switch and eat with virtue just because they've decided it's a good idea. They have emotional issues they need to identify and address before they can eat with true freedom.

That's also true for people who struggle with food or eating addictions. The jury is still out on the nature (and even existence) of food addictions, but good scientific evidence does suggest that some people can get hooked on certain kinds of food (namely refined sugars and complex carbohydrates), much like other people can get hooked on nicotine or alcohol. Over time, the desire to feel the pleasure associated with eating certain foods becomes an actual compulsion, overriding a person's good sense and other desires.

People who truly are addicted to certain foods need to identify their struggle and (to varying degrees) abstain from certain foods before they can regain control and freely make good choices.

All that being said, thinking about eating and the virtues can still be helpful for people who struggle with emotional eating or food addiction.

For starters, justice reminds us to give ourselves our due . . . and sometimes that due is mercy. Those working our way through old wounds or battling compulsions can find, in the call to act justly, a reminder to be gentle and patient with ourselves, just as God, who is always just, is nevertheless also gentle and patient with us. Fortitude can help us face our fears and find the courage to address the underlying problems that give rise to problems with food. Prudence can enable us to seek wise counsel and find someone who can help us confront our struggles head on. Temperance can help us chart a course that will allow us to avoid the foods or situations that create the most problems, so that healing can take place.

Then there's faith, which reminds us to call on God, not just man or our own willpower, for help. Prayer and the sacraments are essential to all real healing. Hope helps us not to get mired in our past failings and temporal struggles, but rather to look to God, whose power is made perfect in our weakness. With God, we can do all things, including overcoming emotional eating and food addictions.

Lastly, charity helps us practice self-forgetfulness, so that our own battles don't entirely consume us. Self-awareness is good. Continuous navel-gazing is not.

SETTING BOUNDARIES:

PRACTICAL TIPS FOR AVOIDING BINGE EATING

When I was working on beating the habit of binging, I set certain rules for myself that helped me immensely. Some of these rules I still follow all the time (Nos. 3, 4, and 5). Others I still generally follow, but not religiously (Nos. 1 and 2). I have better judgment and better habits now than I once did, so the rules aren't quite as important. These may or may not work for you, but regardless, this is what worked for me:

1) Eat every meal sitting down, at a table, with a plate and utensils. No eating standing. No eating out of the carton or boxes.

2) No second helpings. If I want more, I can have it for lunch tomorrow. If there won't be more, that's fine. It's just food. I won't die for the lack of a second helping of it.

3) Never sneak food. Don't hide that I'm eating from family or roommates. Don't do it quietly. Don't eat where I won't be seen.

4) No eating after dinner.

5) No eating sweets by myself. Eat them only with others. And only then on Sundays, special feast days, and birthdays.

* * *

The virtues and eating operate like a two-way street. The benefits flow in both directions.

Exercising our virtues when eating helps us eat well, navigate seasons of fasting and feasting, and make wise choices every day. The virtues also help us maintain the right perspective on food, valuing it and our bodies neither too much nor too little. When we focus on virtuous eating rather than "clean eating," "low-carb eating," "organic eating," or "paleolithic eating," we learn how to nourish our bodies and souls for a lifetime and beyond, not just for thirty days or thirty months or however long some dietary trend lasts.

In turn, eating well helps us become more virtuous. It's a daily workout for our souls where we learn to act justly, discern wisely, do the good in the face of strong temptations to do otherwise, and practice balance, all the while learning to see God's generosity and love in every bite of food we eat.

Ultimately, using our virtues when we sit down to eat makes us free—free to eat, free to cook, free to enjoy the shared community that flourishes best around a meal. It helps us to want the good, know the good, choose the good, and do the good. It's not trendy. It doesn't always make for the pithiest tweets. But it does make for some mighty fine eating . . . with none of the accompanying guilt.

It also makes for much better dinner parties.

ROASTED POTATO, BACON, AND KALE SALAD

Serves: 2

Eating kale doesn't require a great deal of virtue. It just requires bacon.

Ingredients

1 large baking potato, chopped into bite-sized pieces

2 handfuls of green beans, ends snapped off

1 medium-sized sweet onion, thinly sliced

4 strips of bacon

4 handfuls of baby kale

3 tablespoons of olive oil, plus more for dressing the salad

1 tablespoon butter

4–5 large cloves of garlic, peeled and smashed

Freshly grated Pecorino Romano or Parmesan cheese (optional)

Kosher salt

Freshly cracked pepper

Preheat oven to 400° degrees. In a mixing bowl, toss potato pieces with 2 tablespoons of oil, 3 garlic cloves, 2 pinches of salt, and a smattering of pepper. Scatter onto a baking sheet lined with parchment, leaving room at one end for the beans. Place in hot oven and set the timer for 15 minutes. While the potatoes are cooking, fry 4 pieces of bacon on the stove. Set aside, reserving 1 tablespoon of bacon grease. In a mixing bowl, toss the beans, remaining garlic, 1 tablespoon of oil, one pinch of salt, and a smattering of pepper. When the timer goes off, add the beans to the baking sheet in the oven. Cook for 20 minutes more.

While the vegetables continue cooking, heat the reserved bacon grease and the butter in a frying pan; add onion slices and turn the heat down to low. Allow the onions to caramelize, stirring frequently. This should take the full 20 minutes.

When the vegetables are done, assemble the salad. Put about two large handfuls of baby kale on each plate. Evenly divide the potatoes, beans, onions, and bacon and place on top of the kale. Drizzle with olive oil, add a pinch of salt, and top with freshly grated cheese.

CHAPTER TEN

Slaughtering the Fatted Calf
The Gift of Hospitality

A few years after I moved to Steubenville, I bought a house of my own: a 1915 Craftsman that needed restoring from top to bottom. Unlike the couples fixing up homes on HGTV, I didn't have a one hundred thousand dollar restoration fund; I had whatever money was left over from each month's paycheck. Because of that, the restoration process unfolded slowly, taking years, not weeks or months.

Nevertheless, during that time, I continued hosting the weekly dinner parties my roommates and I started throwing during graduate school.

Every Thursday, without fail, twenty-plus friends descended on my house for dinner. I supplied the main dish, while dessert, salad, bread, and wine were brought in by the masses. People ate wherever they could find a seat: in the living room, on the porch, even on the basement floor. It was a happy exercise in chaos, made even more chaotic by constant construction.

If Pinterest were to be believed, not a single person should have shown up for my parties back then. There were no quail eggs laced with truffle oil. People didn't dine off china plates that I hand-painted myself. No crafty mason jar chandeliers hung from the ceiling. Mostly, there was just construction dust, and a lot of it.

Yet those twenty-plus people kept coming back week after week. They ate simple soups and pasta dishes cooked on a decades-old stove in a kitchen that the city probably should have condemned. And they loved every minute of it.

I loved every minute of it too. For me, those Thursday night dinners gave me a chance to show my love for my friends through the food I cooked. Those nights also gave food the chance to do what food does best: create community.

LET ME ENTERTAIN YOU

One of the reasons I started my blog, "The Catholic Table," was to encourage people to open up their homes more frequently to friends. These days, people need that encouragement more than ever. Despite tens of thousands of Pinterest boards dedicated to "entertaining" and the entire industry that is Martha Stewart, fewer and fewer Americans invite their friends over for dinner . . . or drinks . . . or any reason at all anymore.

Between 1980 and the early 2000s, the number of Americans who "entertained people in their homes" on a monthly basis dropped from 40 percent to 20 percent. During the same time period, the number of people who left their homes at least five times a year to dine at friends' homes dropped from 50 percent to 30 percent. As of 2000, fewer than 12 percent of American adults ate in friends' homes at least once a month. More recent data, focused on young adults in their twenties, reports a 40 percent decline over the last decade in the hours they spend socializing in person—as opposed to online—with friends.[1]

---

[1] I found it interesting that while 20 percent of people claimed to entertain monthly, only 12 percent claimed that someone invited them over for a

Experts have posited any number of theories about the "why" behind America's increasingly antisocial behavior: busy schedules, working moms, long commutes, families fractured by distance and divorce. All certainly play their part.

But the very idea of "entertaining" and how it's pitched to us doesn't help.

> "Not everyone has the opportunity to display courage in battle or to show greatness of soul in holding office; but everyone not owned by another is free to give. Everyone with a home can freely invite others to enjoy his hospitality."
>
> LEON KASS, THE HUNGRY SOUL: EATING AND THE
> PERFECTING OF OUR NATURE

PINTEREST PERFECT

If you're contemplating inviting a few friends over for dinner, a few minutes on Pinterest just might convince you otherwise. There, you'll find photo after photo of perfectly plated meals resting on carefully arranged tables in immaculately clean rooms. Click through to the articles those photos represent, and you'll discover headlines like "10 Tricks Every Hostess Should Know," "Last Minute Entertaining Tips That Would Impress Even Martha Stewart," and "How to Throw a Tuscan Inspired Dinner Party."

---

party. Somehow the math doesn't add up. Perhaps people are overestimating how much they entertain, underestimating how often they're entertained, or a bit of both. Claude Fischer, "No Dinner Invitations," Made in America (blog), September 22, 2010, https://madeinamericathebook.wordpress.com/2010/09/22/no-dinner-invitations/; Teddy Wayne, "The Death of the Party," New York Times, September 15, 2015, http://www.nytimes.com/2015/09/17/fashion/death-of-the-party.html.

The articles' purported aim is to help prospective hosts and hostesses. But, in reality, what most of those articles do is simply intimidate them. Today's busy adults can barely manage to get dinner on the table for their own families, let alone find the time to replicate the experience of dining in a rustic Italian garden for thirty of their closest friends. To large swaths of the population, Pinterest-inspired entertaining doesn't sound impossible; it sounds delusional.

The language of the entertaining industry only makes the problem worse.

"With this book, you will always end up with something beautiful that will impress friends and family," promises celebrity chef Sweet Paul's cookbook *Eat and Make*.

"Music can make or break a party," warns Martha Stewart herself in her online "Party Planning Guide."

From Pinterest to *Better Homes and Gardens*, entertaining is primarily depicted as a performance, with the host putting on a show and the guests taking their seats as the appreciative audience. The goal of the performance—whether it's held in a garden illuminated by fairy lights or a spacious, open-concept kitchen with an island big enough to float in the Pacific—is always to impress. The point is to wow others, to elicit praise and admiration. It is, in short, meant to demonstrate to all who walk through our doors how perfectly fabulous we are.

Following that model, entertaining becomes about the hosts, not the guests. It becomes about what we can do—how tasty we can make the food, how beautifully we can set the table, how seamlessly we can make the evening flow. It hinges not on how much love we lavish on our guests, but rather on how much money, time, attention, and skill we lavish on the party.

That kind of hosting comes with a hefty helping of exhaustion, expense, and anxiety, so it's hardly a surprise that fewer and fewer people attempt it (or attempt it on a regular basis). Life is stressful enough. Who needs to worry about whether or not our carefully crafted silver fork place card holders will impress a couple dozen casual acquaintances?

The problem with that mindset, however, is that we're throwing out the proverbial baby with the proverbial bathwater, taking a pass not only on Pinterest Perfect entertaining, but also on practicing genuine Christian hospitality.

EASY PARTY IDEAS

Practicing hospitality doesn't have to mean cooking twelve-course dinners or hosting black tie affairs. Easy ways to open your home to others include:

- Friday Night Movie Nights: Order pizza and watch a show. Or, alternately, order pizza, throw the kids in front of the television to watch a show, and then hang out in the quiet(ish) living room with the grownups, talking and drinking wine.
- Sunday Brunch: Make scones or an egg casserole the night before. Ask everyone to bring something (make sure to assign Bloody Marys and Mimosas to someone), then serve it buffet style after Mass.
- Backyard Cookouts: You supply the meat, everyone else brings sides, drinks, and dessert. Or vice versa.
- Dessert and Drinks: Skip dinner altogether and go straight for the cookies and martinis. Doors open at 7:30 p.m.
- Soup: A pot of soup, a loaf of bread, a bottle of wine, and a crowd of friends. All you need is a roaring fire and you've got the essential ingredients for a perfect night.

- A bourbon tasting (or wine or beer tasting): Everyone brings a bottle. You supply budget-friendly cheeses, meats, crackers, or olives. And glasses. Lots of glasses.

THE ABC'S OF HOSPITALITY

As Christians, we're not called to "entertain" people or put on a show. But we are expected to practice hospitality.

"Show hospitality to one another without grumbling," instructs 1 Peter 4:9.

"Do not neglect to show hospitality to strangers, for thereby some have entertained angels unawares," adds Hebrews 13:2.

Later, in 1 Timothy 5:10, Paul warns that no widow is to be honored unless she has "shown hospitality."

When the biblical writers talk about hospitality, they're not talking about slaughtering a fatted calf for every person who comes calling . . . or laying out a fancy spread of artisanal cheeses and imported olives. What they're talking about is simply opening the doors of our homes and inviting others in—giving the lonely, the lost, the weak, the hungry, the struggling, the searching, the stranger, and the friend an opportunity to experience the love of God through the love we show to them.

That type of hospitality doesn't demand craft cocktails, five star menus, or killer playlists. You can save the party favors for children's birthdays (if then) and ignore the stains on your couch. All you need to practice hospitality is something to eat, something to drink, and a heart willing to love.

SOMETHING TO EAT AND SOMETHING TO DRINK

Food is always a part of hospitality. In Genesis, the first thing Abraham does when strangers come calling is order his servants to prepare food. In the Gospel of Matthew, when Peter's mother is too ill to cook for her guests, Jesus heals her right quick so that she can get back to the kitchen.

The importance of food to hospitality is partly practical. God made us to eat, and if we don't eat, we get weak, tired, and crabby. It's hard for anyone to be at their best if they're hungry, so offering food to guests is a way to tend to both their bodies and their souls. It's a kindness to the whole person. It shows we care about their needs and well-being. It also makes our time with them more enjoyable.

That holds doubly true for drink. If alcoholism runs in your family, you may want to confine your libations to coffee and lemonade. And if you're inviting a few moms over for coffee at 2:00 in the afternoon, nobody expects you to whip out the whisky (although, many might appreciate it if you do). Sometimes, a simple glass of water proffered to a guest is enough refreshment. But I've yet to attend or host a party that wasn't improved by some kind of fermented beverage.

Wine, as the Bible tells us, is a gift from God, given "to gladden the heart of man" (Ps 104:15). It is "like life to man if you drink it in moderation" and it brings "rejoicing of heart and gladness of soul" (Sir 31:27–28). That applies equally to beer and booze, again drunk in moderation. Adult beverages liven a party, elevate a conversation, soothe the weary, relax the stressed, and can do it all while complementing a meal. It just makes hosting (and being hosted) easier.

"God gave us wine to make us gracious and keep us sane."

ROBERT FARRAR CAPON, *THE SUPPER OF THE LAMB:*
A CULINARY REFLECTION

On a deeper level, though, food and drink have a place of honor in Christian hospitality because feeding people is a way of imaging God.

In different times and cultures, good hosts have offered food to their guests as a sign of their generosity. Laying out the best spread possible for whoever came into their home was a way for the host to prove his goodness, wealth, and liberality.

For Christians, feeding guests isn't about proving our own generosity; it's a participation in God's generosity. He gives us good gifts, and we thank him for that by sharing good gifts with others.

Similarly, God shows his love for us by feeding us with his Body and Blood, and we can show our love for others by feeding them with a good risotto and nice Bordeaux. Every meal we serve is an opportunity to show others that they matter, that they are important, that they are worth every minute spent stirring, chopping, and basting.

And ultimately, if all food foreshadows the Eucharist, if what we eat is a natural sign of the supernatural mystery of bread and wine becoming the Body and Blood of Christ, then feeding others is a form of participation in Christ's loving sacrifice.

No sacrifice we can make—in the kitchen or elsewhere—can ever compare to the sacrifice Christ made on the Cross. But hospitality is still a sacrifice. Inviting others into our home always costs us time, money, and occasionally sleep (so many late nights doing dishes . . .). It gives us the chance to die to ourselves for the sake of others. It is an opportunity, in the midst of the daily business of life, to imitate Christ.

One more time: the food we cook and the drinks we serve don't have to be fancy to make love known. They don't have to measure up to the standards of the judges on *Chopped* to be a sacrifice or a sign of God's generosity. Fancy is all well and good, and sometimes, for some of us, it's an awful lot of fun. I do love the chance to use my silver. But it's not essential. It's not even important. When it comes to hospitality, food and drink are a means, not the end. What's important is that something is offered.

What's even more important is the attitude of the person doing the offering.

"God's sharing of food, and self-sharing as food, is the source of divine goodness that heals physical and spiritual hungers, but in addition urges us to share with and care for one another."

ANGEL F. MENDEZ-MONTOYA, *THE THEOLOGY OF FOOD: EATING AND THE EUCHARIST*

A HOST WILLING TO LOVE

The secret to my Thursday night dinners' success was not the food, the booze, or the venue. During the years my house was under construction, I couldn't put on a show if I wanted to. Artisan cocktails and beautifully set tables were the stuff of someone else's life. I had neither the time nor the money to pursue either. If I swept up the dry wall dust before everyone arrived, that was me being classy.

And yet people came back every week. They didn't mind the construction dust. They didn't mind that nothing I served them would win me a James Beard award. All they cared about was that on Thursday nights I gave them a place to belong. They had a community. They had people who would talk with them, laugh with them, and hear about whatever trials and tribulations they'd endured that day. They had my attention, and they had the attention of the other guests. That was enough.

Most of us know that's enough. We know this because we've experienced it. We experienced it as children when the best house in the neighborhood was the house with the big crazy family and a yard strewn with toys. We experience it still, every time a person opens up their house to us and spends the evening talking with us rather than laboring over the meal and dishes in the kitchen. It's not the cleanliness of the baseboards or the clever centerpieces that make an evening. It's a host who looks us in the eye, asks questions, and listens to the answers. It's a host who loves us in a casual, easy way and treats us like we matter.

As a hostess, it's easy to forget this. It's easy to get caught up in the idea of entertaining as performance art, fretting over what people will think about our cooking or our housekeeping and worrying that they'll be overwhelmed by our children, disappointed in dessert, or judgy about our scratched up, wobbly dining room table.

I know it is, because I have to fight that temptation too. I run a Catholic food and hospitality blog, for Pete's sake. New people showing up at my house come with the impression that I'm Julia Child, Martha Stewart, and Mother Teresa rolled into one. Which I most definitely am not. Knowing that, it's tempting to succumb to the pressure of meeting unrealistic expectations and worrying that the reality of me will inevitably disappoint. But if I do that, if I let my hosting become about serving culinary masterpieces in a picture perfect home, I'll either never let people into my home or I'll end up neglecting my most important task as a hostess: loving the people who God sends my way.

That's really what sets hospitality apart from entertaining. A person who is entertaining might serve the same food as someone practicing hospitality. Their house might be just as clean, their booze just as good, and their garden just as lovely under fairy lights. But the person entertaining is focused on impressing people. The person exercising hospitality is focused on loving people. The person entertaining is focused on themselves. The person exercising hospitality is focused on others.

Being a Good Guest

How can you encourage and support those extending hospitality to you? By being a good guest.

- If you receive an invitation to a dinner or party that requires an RSVP, don't dillydally. Get back to the hosts with your answer as soon as you can.

- Don't back out at the last minute unless you have a really good excuse (i.e. the stomach bug has visited your house). Hosts work hard to plan for an event, and honoring your commitments is an act of justice.

- Ask if you can bring something. When in doubt, wine, chocolate, or flowers are almost always welcome.

- If you want to bring a guest with you—a date, a visiting friend, an extra child—give the hostess more than an hour's notice.

- Show up on time. Fashionably late might be fine for a cocktail party, but don't make a hostess hold dinner for you.

- Make conversation with others. Ask questions. Talk to new people. Even if this means going out of your comfort zone.

- Offer to help clean up at the end of the night. Your hostess will most likely say no . . . unless it's me doing the hosting.
- Say thank you. You don't have to write a formal thank you note the next day (although, those are always fun to receive), but do thank the hosts when you're leaving or with a quick phone call or email the next day. The hard work of hosting is made lighter when it's appreciated.

That distinction should be at the forefront of our minds when preparing to ask others into our homes. As Christians, we're not supposed to invite friends and co-workers over for dinner to show off our immaculate baseboards and crystal wine glasses. We're supposed to invite them over to laugh with them, tell stories with them, and get to know them better. The goal is to strengthen old friendships and forge new ones. It's to show people that they matter, they're important, and they're worthy of being known and loved.

You don't need a big, beautiful house to accomplish that. If it comes down to it, you don't even need a clean house. You just need a generous spirit, a loving heart, and an attentive ear. If you have those things, the dust bunnies, chipped dishes, and toddlers decorating the dining room with spaghetti sauce just add to your charm.

* * *

Right now, each of us has a neighbor, co-worker, or friend eating dinner alone. There's also a newly-married couple or newly-arrived family in our parish feeling lost and overwhelmed. Or maybe it's you eating alone, you waiting for the dinner invitation to come.

We need to stop waiting and invite someone over to join us. It doesn't have to be twenty people. It can be just one. It's okay to start small. It's okay to keep it simple.

It also doesn't matter if walls are covered with little kids' hand-prints, if furniture dates back to the Carter Administration, or if the best dinner we can muster up is grilled cheese and tomato soup served on paper plates. That's okay. What matters is simply you—your love, your attentiveness, your desire to make your guests part of your life, even for just a little while. Hospitality doesn't require a lot of money or a lot of skill. It just requires a lot of you.

All that being said, there's nothing wrong with handmade ma-son jar chandeliers. If you like making that stuff, great. Go for it. If quail eggs in truffle oil are your specialty, that's fine too. Serve them up. Heck, if it makes you happy, use the silver while you're at it. It certainly does me.

And yes, it's good to tidy up the house a bit before guests ar-rive . . . at least clearing the bills off the dining room table and the laundry off the living room couch. A place for guests to sit helps.

But as we do all that, we mustn't make the mistake of thinking those details are the essence of hospitality. They're not. The essence is love, kindness, and respect. The essence is simply giving people a space where they can come to know others and be known by others. That's what makes for a successful dinner party and al-lows community to grow.

That's what gives people a foretaste of the supper to which we're all invited: the marriage supper of the Lamb.

Baked Tortellini with Pesto, Sun-Dried Tomato, and Cheese

Serves 6

In the early, somewhat delusional stages of wedding planning, I wanted to cook our rehearsal dinner. We eventually realized that would be an exercise in madness and made reservations at a foodie burger joint instead. Had we continued to live dangerously, however, this is what I would have served. Impossibly easy and extremely impressive, you can make it hours (or even a day) ahead of time, then bake it in the oven 30 minutes before it's time to eat. Which makes it the perfect dinner for company . . . if not for self-catered rehearsal dinners.

Ingredients

2 bags frozen tortellini

8 ounces basil pesto

6 ounces sun-dried tomatoes, drained and sliced

½ cup pine nuts

1 15-ounce can of black olives, sliced

8 ounces sliced Provolone cheese

In a medium-sized frying pan, lightly toast pine nuts over medium heat. When they begin to brown, remove from pan and set aside. In another large pot, bring water to boil. Add tortellini and cook according to package instructions. Drain and place tortellini in a large baking dish.

Stir in pesto, sun-dried tomatoes, olives, and pine nuts. Combine well. Top with sliced Provolone. Then, either refrigerate until ready to cook or bake at 350° for 20–25 minutes or until the dish is heated through and the cheese has melted.

CHAPTER ELEVEN

Kitchen Rules
A Practical Theology of Food

I
t has been twenty years since I sat in a college classroom exhausted, famished, and frantically calculating calories on my notebooks. It has been almost sixteen years since I walked back to my pew with God on my tongue and a new understanding of food in my heart. And it's been eleven years since Eucharistic eating—eating gratefully and joyfully, nourishing my body and my soul—became a comfortable, settled habit for me.

Note the five-year gap between understanding and habit.

Intellectually, my healing happened in an instant. Practically, it took several years of trial and error. Just as my metabolism had to reset itself after years of deprivation, so did my mind. I had to break engrained patterns of thought about food and acquire new ones.

I also had to learn what types of foods and amounts of food my body really needed. I spent years ignoring its demands, and in the process I stopped understanding it. Hunger and fullness were difficult experiences to navigate. I needed to relearn what both meant and adjust my eating accordingly.

Above all, I had a lot of spiritual unpacking to do. Through the sacraments and the theology of the body, God taught me that everything I did in my body, including eating, was a chance to grow closer to him. He showed me the big picture. But understanding all the little pictures—the daily application of the overarching truth about food—took years of thinking, praying, writing, and just doing. It took feasting and fasting; cooking for myself and cooking for others; eating kale and eating cheesecake; knowing the whole while that all the "doing" was important and sacred, but sometimes only doing it as a matter of obedience.

It was through that obedience, more than anything else, that I came to understand the full depth of food's import and sacredness. I did the good things I knew I was supposed to do; a deeper understanding of those good things followed.

Today, I call those good things my "Kitchen Rules." Early on, they helped me make good choices that reflected a sacramental understanding of food. When I was tempted to eat less-than-Eucharistically—less-than-gratefully, less-than-joyfully, less-than-virtuously, or in some way that didn't nourish my body and soul—they helped me overcome that temptation.

They still do. When I'm tired, stressed, or anxious, and old thought patterns momentarily rear their ugly heads, these rules call me back to sanity. They remind me where the grace lies, where the peace lies. They also help me navigate the ever-changing food landscape. As new diet trends come and go, they set unchanging truth before me.

In sum, my "Kitchen Rules" are the practical application of all we've talked about thus far in this book. They are how I live what I preach.

There are nine of them.

1. EAT JOYFULLY

Food is not something to be feared. It's something to be enjoyed. Food was given to us by God to nourish us, nurture us, teach us, console us, comfort us, delight us, and draw us together. It is a gift. It is a blessing. It is a means of grace. And you don't fear grace. You don't weigh it, measure it, and calculate it. You receive it. You delight in it. You relish it, giving praise and glory to God with every sip of wine you imbibe and every plate of pasta in which you partake.

God's love for us—his generous, gratuitous, abundant love—is in every bite and every morsel of every meal we consume. Enjoy the love. Savor it. Share it with others. There will always be more than enough to go around.

2. EAT GRATEFULLY

As you enjoy the gift of food, give thanks for it. Praise God for every broccoli stalk and Brussels sprout, every coffee bean and lima bean. It's all good. Even beets . . . somehow.

God didn't have to make food taste so good. But he did. God didn't have to make food so abundant. But he did. God didn't have to order the universe and arrange human events in such a manner that a steaming bowl of lamb curry is sitting in front of you right now. But he did. And he deserves to be thanked for it.

So, say grace at every meal. Say it while you're rushing out the door, breakfast sandwich in hand. Say it while you're sitting at your desk, sipping a steaming café mocha. Say it at night, when you sit down with your family or when you sit down alone. Say it in public too. Be a witness in the restaurant or the park to the truth that all good things, including all tasty things, come from God.

3. EAT LITURGICALLY

Fast when the Church fasts. Pray more during Advent and save the cookies for Christmas. Give up sweets during Lent. Or lattes. Or booze. Also abstain from meat every Friday between Ash Wednesday and Easter Sunday. Fast from meat on Fridays year-round, if possible. The Church still calls us to make a voluntary sacrifice every Friday, and meat is the sacrifice she most highly recommends.

Then, when the Church feasts, feast with her. Have dessert on Sunday—every Sunday. Buy an extra special bottle of wine for Christmas Day or for your favorite saint's feast day. Celebrate Name Days and Baptismal anniversaries, eat a piece of chocolate every single day during Easter, and definitely eat bacon on the Fridays that fall during the Octaves of Christmas and Easter (and on solemnities that fall on Fridays too). A failure to feast isn't something we have to confess. We don't *have* to dine on steak on Easter Friday. But as a wise man once told me, "You can fast when the Church is feasting. But know that you fast alone."

"Every real thing is a joy, if only you have eyes and ears to relish it, a nose and tongue to taste it."

ROBERT FARRAR CAPON, THE SUPPER OF THE LAMB:
A CULINARY REFLECTION

---

4. EAT VIRTUOUSLY

When you eat, bring the cardinal virtues to the dinner table with you. Practice temperance by eating one cookie, not three. Exercise prudence by taking a larger portion of spinach and a smaller portion of garlic mashed potatoes. Grow in fortitude by making those hard choices every day, not just once in a while. And become more just by seeking to give your body, which is a temple of the Holy Spirit, its due (but not at the expense of your budget, the poor, or those who host you for a meal or two).

In sum, see every meal as an opportunity to become more the person God made you to be. And see the natural virtues God gave you—not some silly fad diet or a bottle of suspect pills—as the most effective tools at your disposal for helping you stay healthy and strong.

5. EAT COMMUNALLY

Turn off the television. Silence your phone. Set the table. Call the kids and your spouse into the dining room. Then, dine. Look one another in the eye. Ask questions. Listen. Respond. Tell stories. Teach manners. Laugh. Create memories. Invite others to join you, too—the single co-worker, the elderly neighbor, the new family from the parish, all of them. Practice hospitality indiscriminately. Remember, for Christians it's obligatory, not optional.

The same holds true if you're single. Invite a friend (or twenty) to join you for Wednesday night supper. Order pizza if you can't cook. Grill in your backyard on Saturdays. Go out for brunch on Sundays. Lunch dates and coffee dates can counteract too many weeknight suppers eaten alone, and the friendships that blossom over a hot pot of soup will see you through the hardest and darkest moments of your years alone.

6. EAT OMNIVOROUSLY

God knew what he was doing when he made eggs . . . and walnuts . . . and the magical little animal that gives us bacon, ham, sausage, and pork. He knew what the human body needed to be nourished.

He also knew what the human soul needed to be nourished. Accordingly, he created a world full of tasty and nutritious foods perfectly designed to nourish body and soul. To make eating those foods possible, he then gave us taste buds that could appreciate a wide variety of foods, teeth that could chew a wide variety of foods, and stomachs that could digest a wide variety of foods.

Use what God gave you.

Eat your veggies; they're best roasted. Eat fat; it gives you energy, improves bone and muscle strength, bolsters your immune system, and does any number of other good things for your body. Drink your milk whole; if God wanted milk to be tasteless blue water, he would have made it that way. The same goes for cheese; fat-free cheese is an abomination. If John the Evangelist had known about it, it would have gotten its own chapter in Revelation. Don't be afraid of bacon; bacon is proof that God is good. Dessert has its place in every healthy diet; I like mine full of dairy and on Sundays. And grains are not the bogeyman; they supply us with all sorts of important nutrients and serve as a necessary ingredient in some of the world's tastiest foods—scones, pizza, cookies.

PATRON SAINTS OF COOKING:

HONORÉ OF FRANCE

As a child, the sixth-century French bishop St. Honoré acted less-than-saintly. He acted less-than-priestly too. So much so that when his childhood nurse learned that the Church had made her former charge a bishop, she refused to believe it. The nurse was in the midst of baking bread at the time, and announced that she would only believe Honoré had become a bishop if the bread paddle in her hand turned into a tree.

At that very moment, the paddle fell from her hands, planted itself into the ground, and sprouted up into a blackberry tree. Within seconds, luscious, ripe fruit dangled from its branches.

That convinced the nurse. As the years went by, it also made St. Honoré revered among bakers. They eventually established their guild at the cathedral built in his honor, and to this day Paris celebrates his feast day with a three-day festival of bread. Year round, you can also purchase tasty cakes in France's bakeries which bear the saint's name: Gâteau St. Honoré, puff pastry cream puffs filled with pastry cream and topped with caramelized sugar.

Yum.

---

7. EAT CHARITABLY

Food is love. And the food others make for us is a sign of their love for us. They sacrificed their time, money, and energy to put that heaping plate of mashed potatoes in front of you. And unless mashed potatoes make you break out in hives, you need to eat those potatoes with a smile on your face and a "thank you" on your lips.

There's nothing wrong with having preferences. We all have them. Personally, I think beets are the stuff of horror shows. At my own house, at my own table, you will not find beets. But, if that's what's for dinner at your house, I'm going to eat beets and be grateful, because your hard work and your kindness in serving me matters more than my personal tastes.

Pickiness, you'll recall, is not a virtue. It's a sin. Being overly particular about what we eat makes an idol of our appetites and preferences. Our likes and dislikes become our god, and others—those cooking for us, serving us, or shopping for us—must worship at the same altar. Ultimately, pickiness is a failure of charity. It fails to adequately appreciate the gift of another.

So, don't be picky. Try new things. Expand your horizons. And eat what you're served. Unless it actually will kill you. Then, by all means, take a pass. Do try, however, to inform hosts and hostesses about food allergies before you sit down at their table. Again, for charity's sake.

Also, be wary of non-medically necessary diets that separate you from the community or make it difficult for you to eat easily with others. Avoiding allergens or following a doctor's orders is a necessary cross. Voluntarily choosing to eliminate whole food groups from your diet is an unnecessary one. It can erect a divide between you and your loved ones, and make hosting you or cooking for you unnecessarily burdensome. Freely chosen crosses are all well and good in their place. We should all have some. But when we're choosing crosses, it's best to just choose our own, not foist them on the people we love.

SHOULD CATHOLICS BE VEGETARIANS?

Can Catholics be vegetarians? Sure. The Church doesn't mandate Catholics eat meat, and plenty of holy men and women through the centuries have foregone animal flesh as a form of penance. It's a good one.

But *should* Catholics be vegetarians? Or, for that matter, vegans? Frankly, that's a question for individuals and their spiritual directors. For some people, the answer will be yes. But other people should think twice before foregoing bacon forever.

The desert fathers and medieval mystics who practiced vegetarianism usually lived by themselves, in isolation from others. Their vegetarianism imposed nothing on anyone. It demanded nothing of others. For lay people living in the world, however, the decision to eat in a dramatically different way from friends and family can be an imposition and a frustration. It also can cause rifts in relationships if it makes it difficult for the people who love you to cook for you.

There's also a question of health. While sometimes the best thing you can do for your body may be giving up animal products (evidence suggests a vegan diet may benefit those fighting cancer), many people struggle to get all the nutrition they need from plants. If you're pressed for time, money, or cooking skills, eating meat may make eating healthy easier.

Lastly, if you've ever struggled with an eating disorder, exercise extreme caution about going vegetarian or vegan. First, because it encourages a restrictive mindset. Second, because many recovering anorexics use vegetarianism to mask ongoing eating issues. It can become just another way to exercise control over food.

Ultimately, the decision to embrace a meatless diet is up to you and God. What really matters is not whether you become a vegetarian, but how you go about living as a vegetarian. The best vegetarians don't lecture others about eating meat (because the Church doesn't). They don't make a fuss about their choices. They let their hosts know about their meatless status beforehand. And they usually offer to bring a vegetarian side dish to add to the fare. As in all things, what matters is charity and humility. If you can give up meat without giving up those virtues, you're golden.

---

8. EAT NATURALLY

God made us to eat meals, not meal replacements. A diet that has us primarily getting our nutrition from a package—whether that package is a high-powered protein shake or a Hungry-Man Frozen

Dinner—is a diet lacking in variety, flavor, creativity, community, and ultimately joy. It also can be a sign of disorder—of a schedule or life that is busier and more distracted than it needs to be for true human flourishing.

That's not to say it's a sin to substitute the occasional nutrition shake for your breakfast. And there are definitely worse things than an Amy's Frozen Burrito now and then. Sometimes, eating prepackaged foods is the most practical, efficient thing to do. For some, it also might be the first step towards eating healthier. But it shouldn't be the last step. If God wanted us eating PowerBars for breakfast, lunch, and dinner, he would have made PowerBars grow on trees. But he didn't. He made apples grow on trees.

So, eat more apples and fewer apple-flavored PowerBars. Eat more lentils and fewer protein shakes. Eat more soups that come off the stove and avoid the ones that come out of cans. Likewise, at the grocery store, buy fresh foods with ingredients you can pronounce and which don't come in individually sized microwavable containers. Or better yet, buy ingredients—tomatoes, garlic, onions, olive oil—and put them in your own individually sized microwavable containers. We call these bowls.

"An immature palate turns away the multiple gifts God wants to provide. It rejects different formational experiences that can help shape one's view of the world and the role one plays in it, including the role one plays in salvation history."

FR. LEO PATALINGHUG, *EPIC FOOD FIGHT:
A BITE-SIZED HISTORY OF SALVATION*

---

9. EAT WISELY

Use commonsense wisdom in how you think about your food, your eating habits, and yourself.

First, remember, there are no good foods and bad foods. There are yummy foods and icky foods, healthy foods and less-than-healthy foods, special treat foods and everyday foods. But food does not have a moral value. It is not capable of virtue or vice. It is a thing. It can't earn gold stars in heaven or go to confession.

Likewise, you are not good or bad because of what you eat. Having a piece of pie after supper, cooking with olive oil instead of coconut oil, or buying your toddler nephew graham crackers laden with GMOs does not make you "bad." Nor does having a kale salad for lunch, drinking twenty-dollar-a-pound free trade coffee, and eating nothing but hormone-free meat make you "good." Holiness has nothing to do with what you cooked for dinner last night. Your moral rectitude is not determined by the food in your pantry, where you shop, or who grew your corn. It's determined by whether or not you are patient in traffic, kind to the checker at the grocery store, generous to your neighbor, faithful to your spouse, and grateful to God, loving him by doing his will.

Also, eat when you're hungry, stop when you're full. If you're bored, skip the Oreos and clean your toilet instead. If you're depressed, have a talk with Jesus, not Ben and Jerry. You don't have to eat the donuts Marjory from Accounting brought in just because they're there. And the clean plate club does not accept adults for membership; we can save what we don't eat for tomorrow.

Last but not least, remember that it's better to be a happy, healthy, energetic size 6 (or 8 or 10 or 12), than it is to be a crabby, crotchety, underfed size 2. Life is short—too short for not eating creamy bowls of risotto, pizza dripping with cheese, and salted caramel cheesecake with a crispy graham cracker crust. Likewise, Christmas parties are a thousand times more fun when you're drinking cocktails and dining on bacon wrapped dates, not munching on celery in a corner. And what is a birthday without cake?

Each of us only has so many hours left on this planet. In those hours, we have babies to chase, houses to clean, races to run, cities to tour, spouses to kiss, walls to paint, poems to read, gardens to plant, horses to ride, mountains to climb, ponds to fish, baseballs to throw, parties to host, homeless to feed, children to dress, symphonies to hear, books to write, buildings to design, cars to drive, stories to tell, friends to make, bodies to heal, and souls to save. There's no time to count calories. There's no time to fret about stretch marks and cellulite. There's no time to waste being hungry and tired.

At the end of our life, the size of our jeans won't matter. The value of our days won't hinge on how much we weighed. It will hinge on how much we loved. So, take care of yourself. Be healthy. Be strong. Eat your vegetables. It makes all that living and loving easier. But don't waste precious minutes trying to get to an "ideal" weight if your real weight is just fine. Never forget: the body is not a god to worship, it's a temple to be cared for.

* * *

And that's how I roll. It's not brain surgery. It doesn't require a degree in theology or a will of iron. It's just a simple matter of putting my faith into practice at the table.

Over time, eating Eucharistically has become, for me, a simple matter of habit. I'm not tempted to eat my feelings anymore. I'm not tempted to restrict my calories or axe entire food groups from my menu. Nor am I tempted to eat a steady diet of fried mozzarella sticks and bacon cheeseburgers. Remember, I'm the woman who thinks Brussels sprouts are comfort food. At the same time, I also don't feel guilty when I do have the occasional fried mozzarella stick or bacon cheeseburger. It's all good. It's all really good. And for that, I'm grateful.

Again, though, this habit wasn't formed overnight. It took time. It took effort. And it took prayer. Sometimes I didn't follow my own rules. I had rough patches along the way. That's part of the journey. But that's okay. The journey is a good one. Especially when it includes cheese.

PUMPKIN CHEESECAKE

Serves 8–12

If everything good and loved is lifted up into the marriage supper of the Lamb, there's no way this pumpkin cheesecake isn't on the menu.

Ingredients

2 cups gingersnap cookie crumbs

1 stick butter, melted

24 ounces cream cheese (room temperature)

1 15-ounce can pumpkin puree

3 eggs, plus 1 egg yolk

¼ cup sour cream

1½ cups sugar

½ teaspoon cinnamon

¼ teaspoon nutmeg

⅛ teaspoon ground cloves

2 tablespoons flour

1 teaspoon vanilla extract

Preheat oven to 350° degrees. Combine gingersnap crumbs and butter in a bowl. Mix well, until crumbs are moist. Pour into the bottom of a 9-inch springform pan and press until firm.

Using a stand mixer, beat cream cheese until smooth. Add sour cream, pumpkin, eggs, egg yolk, and sugar. Beat until combined. Add spices. Beat some more. Lastly, add vanilla and flour. Beat until the mixture is uniformly smooth, stopping once or twice to scrape the bottom of the bowl if necessary.

Pour into the pan. Place in the oven on the center rack. Beneath it, place a 9x13 pan, half-filled with water. Bake for one hour. When finished, turn oven off, and prop the oven door open for 10–15 minutes. Remove from oven and let sit on the counter for 10–15 minutes more. Cover tightly with saran wrap and refrigerate overnight.

The Food that Heals

B ooks have the strangest habit of taking on a life of their own. At the outset, you think you know what you want to say and how you want to say it, but somewhere along the way, that inevitably changes.

For example, when I set out to write *The Catholic Table*, I wasn't planning on talking quite so much about my history with food. I planned on a chapter of that and no more. But, as the writing progressed, it became clear that I couldn't separate my story from my theology and practice. It was all of a piece. One didn't make sense without explaining the other.

Reflecting on that now, I see why. Food is such an intimate part of our lives. We can't get away from it. It's there every morning, noon, and night, as well as during so many of the hours in between. It's there when we keep company with family and friends. And it's there at every important milestone in our lives: births, Baptisms, First Holy Communions and Confirmations, when we marry, and when we die.

Food is part of our story—as a culture, as a family, as individuals. So, naturally, my thoughts on food are bound up with my own story. Your story will be different. Your experiences will be different. That doesn't change the importance or the meaning of food. It just means we'll all struggle and progress in different ways and at a different pace. It also means that some habits and practices that I found profoundly helpful, like not snacking or only eating sweets in the company of others, might be less helpful for you.

Likewise, because the ways in which many of us struggle with food are different, some aspects of the healing process will be different too. Moving towards a place of wholeness and freedom with food requires wisdom and discernment. This book shouldn't be a substitute for that, but rather a helpful guide in the process.

And it is a process.

Every occasion for celebration and mourning, every gathering, every day, food is there. It's woven into the fabric of our lives like few other things. For people who struggle with food, that makes it a unique problem. Alcoholics can give up alcohol entirely. Nicotine addicts can choose to not smoke another cigarette. Sex addicts can swear off pornography. But you can't swear off food. You have to eat and you have to go places where others eat. You have to cook for others and eat what others cook.

Navigating our way out of unhealthy, negative, or sinful eating habits takes time. Minds can change overnight, but hearts and habits rarely do. It took me almost five years of understanding the truth about food before I could fully live that truth. And I'm someone who typically excels at doing what I set out to do. I'm a highly disciplined Type A choleric. So, if it still took me five years to completely get my act together regarding eating, don't expect to beat all your bad habits by next week. Be gentle and merciful with yourself. Be gentle and merciful with others too.

That being said, there are a few things you can do to help the healing process along.

First, believe it's possible. To some of you that may sound self-evident, but over the years I've spoken with so many men and women who think they can't change how they eat. They believe God can become man, die, rise from the dead, and come back to us in the form of a piece of bread, but they don't believe that God can help them discipline their sweet tooth or overcome their fear of fat.

Don't think that way. Don't underestimate God. What he wants for each of us is wholeness. He wants holiness. He wants us to be the people he made us to be and see the world as he made it to be seen. He wants you to delight in every good thing in this world, beets included. And his grace is great enough to make that happen.

Yes, it might take longer than you like. Yes, there might be some thorns that remain in your side right up to the very end. Maybe a plate of cookies will always be your downfall. That's just the way it goes in a fallen world. Besides, God is God and he knows best. He has his purposes. But to deny the possibility of healing from eating disorders, disordered eating, food addictions, or gluttony is to deny the reality of God's grace. And that's a bad idea.

Second, remember the words of Ash Wednesday: "From dust you came, to dust you shall return."

No matter how many green smoothies we drink, our days on earth are still numbered. All the healthy eating in the world won't keep us alive forever. It might not even keep us alive until next week. A speeding bus or crashing plane might render our Whole 30 fast moot.

Yes, of course, it's good to eat well. It's good and important and necessary to care for our bodies. But death is going to get us just the same. One hundred years ago, people might not have worried about gluten or pesticides or antibiotics poisoning them. But they did worry about yellow fever . . . or dying in childbirth if their baby was breach . . . or losing their arm (and subsequently their life) on a factory floor. It's all kind of a wash. Which is why some of us just need to chill a little when it comes to worrying about what we put into our bodies. That, at least, is what I tell myself every time I start to get too precious by half about what I'm eating. It helps me remember that any extra years hyper-focusing on food might buy me aren't worth living if that hyper-focusing causes me to fail in charity, generosity, or humility. Better to die a saint, I figure, than live as a massive pain in the tuckus. Better to leave this earth with a body full of GMOs and a heart full of love than live on in an empty house with a bitter spirit.

Food is supposed to help get us to heaven, not keep us out. So, priorities: keep 'em straight.

Finally, if you want to help the healing process along, get yourself to the Eucharist as often as possible. Receive Jesus in Holy Communion. Kneel before him in Eucharistic Adoration. Place yourself in his presence and you will be transformed. That is a guarantee.

A year or so back, my neighbor and I were chatting about the Eucharist. Because that neighbor is Catholic theologian Dr. Scott Hahn, he says some pretty smart things.

"People," he told me, "have more faith in Tylenol than they do in the Eucharist."

He's right.

When we have a headache or backache, we run straightaway to the medicine cabinet and pop open a bottle of pills. But when we're lost, confused, or in need of spiritual healing, so few of us run to the nearest tabernacle with the same confidence. We forget that small white Host contains a healing power infinitely greater than the healing power in any pill. But it does. There is greater grace in Christ's Eucharistic presence than our created minds can begin to fathom. And if we would only avail ourselves more often of that grace, not only would we change, but the whole world would change.

Probably the single most important thing I did during those first years of my recovery was go to Daily Mass and regular Eucharistic Adoration. I received Christ on my tongue and sat my body before his Body, over and over again. While I sat there, I contemplated what it meant to eat Eucharistically. Resting before the One who becomes food for me, I thought about food. And bit by bit, a Eucharistic understanding of food replaced my worldly understanding of food. Likewise, a sacramental understanding of my body replaced my materialist understanding of my body.

Christ as food, Christ as Body transformed every part of me. His Eucharistic self renewed my mind, just like St. Paul promised. He healed me and made me whole, introducing me to a world where eating wasn't fraught with anxiety, but enlivened by joy. He also introduced me to a world of culinary and communal delights— of long, late nights sipping Scotch with friends, of happy evenings dancing and cooking in the kitchen with roommates, of hours spent learning the ways of risotto and polenta, pork belly and lamb biryani, coffee-infused birthday cakes, Nutella-laced brownies, and Beemster goat cheeses.

In his great mercy, God took pity on me and made a place for me at the Catholic table. And if you give him enough time and enough opportunities, he will do the same for you.

There's always room.

Bibliographic Essay

CHAPTER 1: UNCLEAN—SURVEYING AMERICA'S FOOD LANDSCAPE

There are dozens of books on the market today that explore America's ever-evolving palate, as well as the dangers of both our culture's diet and the food industry. Some are interesting; others are alarmist.

The most important reads, however, include Michael Pollen's books *The Omnivore's Dilemma: A Natural History of Four Meals* (London: Penguin, 2007) and *In Defense of Food: An Eater's Manifesto* (London: Penguin, 2009), as well as *Fast Food Nation: The Dark Side of the All-American Meal* by Erik Schlosser (Boston: Houghton Mifflin Company, 2001).

Margaret Visser's books on food and food culture are a wonderful read, more historical in nature, but excellent at capturing food and eating trends over time. They include *Much Depends on Dinner: The Extraordinary History and Mythology, Allure and Obsessions, Perils and Taboos of an Ordinary Meal* (New York: Grove Press, 1988) and *The Rituals of Dinner: The Origins, Evolution, Eccentricities and Meaning of Table Manners* (London: Penguin, 1991).

From a Catholic perspective, Fr. Leo Patalinghug has done wonderful work for many years now trying to bring back the family dinner. His short essays, included in his cookbook *Grace Before Meals: Recipes and Inspiration for Family Meals and Family Life* (New York: Image Books, 2010), are well worth a read.

CHAPTER 2: WASTELAND—MY HUNGRY YEARS

One of the first books I recommend to anyone who is struggling to understand anorexia or bulimia is Peggy Claude-Pierre's *The Secret Language of Eating Disorders: How You Can Understand and Work to Cure Anorexia and Bulimia* (New York: Random House, 1997). I read it at the height of my own battle with anorexia, and of all the books I read on the topic, it was the only secular book that accurately described what I was feeling and experiencing (and the only one I recommend). Over the years, as I've talked with other young women fighting similar battles, the language they use to describe their struggles echoes Claude-Pierre's. Her insights are deep and real.

Specifically Catholic books on eating disorders and disordered eating that are very worth reading include *Weightless* by Kate Wicker (Cincinnati: Servant, 2011), *Cravings: A Catholic Wrestles with Food, Self-Image, and God* by Mary DeTurris Poust (Notre Dame, IN: Ave Maria Press, 2012), and *Hunger for Freedom* by Katie Gesto (Maitland, FL: Xulon Press, 2004).

CHAPTER 3: REALITY RE-ENCHANTED— SEEING THE WORLD WITH CATHOLIC EYES

If you want to read more about the sacramental worldview, I can't think of anyone better to read than G. K. Chesterton. In both his non-fiction and fiction he does a better job of capturing the mystery and wonder of creation than just about anyone else. For non-fiction, a good place to start is *Orthodoxy* (New York: John Lane Company, 1908), which was actually written when Chesterton was still an Anglican. For fiction, I have a soft spot for *The Poet and the Lunatics* (London: Cassell, 1929), but his *Father Brown* mysteries are probably more accessible.

Beyond Chesterton, some of the books that have formed my sacramental worldview most profoundly include Karl Adam's *The Spirit of Catholicism* (New York: Image Books, 1964), Frank Sheed's *Theology and Sanity* (San Francisco: Ignatius Press, 1993), Tom Howard's *Chance or the Dance* (San Francisco: Ignatius Press, 1969), and Fr. James Schall's *On the Unseriousness of Human Affairs* (Wilmington, DE: ISI Books, 2001).

Fiction writers do an even better job, I think, of capturing the essence of the sacramental worldview. Georges Bernanos' *Diary of a Country Priest* (Cambridge, MA: Da Capo Press, 1964), Francois Mauriac's *Woman of the Pharisees* (New York: Carroll & Graf, 1993), Sigrid Undset's *Kristin Lavransdatter* (London: Penguin, 2005) and *Master of Hestviken* (New York: Vintage Books, 1994) cycles (I prefer the latter even more than the former), and Flannery O'Connor's short stories should all be required reading for anyone trying to grasp how grace works in a life and in the world.

For understanding the world's progression from a sacramental worldview to a modernist worldview, I highly recommend the works of Christopher Dawson, especially *The Crisis of Western Education* (Steubenville, OH: Franciscan University Press, 1989), *The Dynamics of World History* (New York: Mentor Omega Books, 1962), and *The Making of Europe* (Cleveland: The World Publishing Company, 1961). Dr. Scott Hahn has a forthcoming book on the mystery of faith that also contains an excellent analysis on the progression of modernism. His view has, I admit, almost thoroughly formed mine, thanks both to my studies under him in the classroom and my work with him in the years since.

For books more focused on the twentieth century, John Lukacs'
*A New Republic: A History of the United States in the Twentieth
Century* (London: Yale University Press, 2004) and *A Thread of
Years* (London: Yale University Press, 1998) are both fascinating
and beautiful reads. Paul Johnson's *Modern Times: The World from
the Twenties to the Nineties* (New York: HarperCollins, 2001) is
even more accessible, if slightly less poetic, than Lukacs' books.

CHAPTER 4: OUR DAILY BREAD—FOOD AS SIGN AND SACRAMENT

If you're going to read one book about food and faith (besides this
one of course), it should be Robert Farrar Capon's *The Supper of
the Lamb: A Culinary Reflection* (New York: Doubleday, 1969). I
first read it in 2002 and didn't realize until I went back through
it prior to writing this book just how profoundly his understanding of food shaped mine. His prose on the splendor of onions and
bread reads more like poetry, and anyone would be hard pressed to
read this book and not have his view of food transformed.

Leon Kass' *The Hungry Soul: Eating and the Perfecting of Our
Natures* (Chicago: University of Chicago Press, 1994) does an
excellent job unpacking the natural truths about food. Fr. Angel
Mendez-Montoya's *The Theology of Food: Eating and the Eucharist*
(Hoboken, NJ: Wiley Blackwell, 2012), Ann Astell's *Eating Beauty:
The Eucharist and the Spiritual Arts of the Middle Ages* (Ithaca, NY:
Cornell University, 2006), and Cristina Mazzoni's *The Women in
God's Kitchen* (London: Bloomsbury Academic, 2006) offer more
academic studies of the relationship between food and faith.

CHAPTER 5: THE BODY BEAUTIFUL—
A THEOLOGY OF THE BODY

There are so many good books out there now on St. John Paul II's anthropology it's hard to know where to begin. Obviously, it's a good thing to read the catechesis itself. Michael Waldstein's translation, published as *Man and Woman He Created Them: A Theology of the Body* (Boston: Pauline Books and Media, 2006), is far better than the original translation I read back in 2001.

Study guides that serve as good companions while reading the pope's work include Mary Healy's *Men and Women are from Eden* (Cincinnati: St. Anthony Messenger, 2005) and Anastasia Northrop's *The Freedom of the Gift* (Our Father's Will Communications).

Books which do an excellent job of unpacking John Paul II's dense, cyclical writing at a basic level are *Theology of the Body Made Simple* by Fr. Anthony Percy (Boston: Pauline Books and Media, 2006); *Theology of the Body for Beginners*, revised edition, by Christopher West (West Chester, PA: Ascension Press, 2009); *Men, Women and the Mystery of Love: Practical Insights from John Paul II's Love and Responsibility* by Dr. Edward Sri (Cincinnati: Servant Press, 2007); and *Sex Au Natural* by Patrick Coffin (Steubenville, OH: Emmaus Road, 2009).

One of my personal favorites on the topic is Sr. Mary Timothy Prokes' *Toward a Theology of the Body* (Grand Rapids, MI: Eerdmans, 1996). *The Christian Meaning of Human Sexuality* by Fr. Paul Quay (San Francisco: Ignatius Press, 1988), *Crossing the Threshold of Love: A New Vision of Marriage* by Mary Shivanandan (Washington, DC: CUA Press, 1999), and Fr. Benedict Ashley's *Theologies of the Body: Humanist and Christian* (St. Louis: The Pope John Center, 1985) are also excellent, as is Susan Windley-Daoust's *Theology of the Body Extended: The Spiritual Signs of Birth, Impairment, and Dying* (Hobe Sound, FL: Lectio Publishing, 2014).

CHAPTER 6: BREAD FROM HEAVEN—FOOD IN SACRED SCRIPTURE

Books on food and Scripture are surprisingly few and far between. There may be some scholarly books or Protestant books out there on the topic, but I haven't seen them. Fr. Leo Patalinghug's *Epic Food Fight: A Bite-Sized History of Salvation* (Cincinnati: Servant, 2014), however, is an exception to that. It's a fascinating and easy read that looks at salvation history through the lens of food.

Dr. Scott Hahn's work on the covenants, the Eucharist, the Passover, and the *Todah* are foundational reading for the role of food in salvation history. *The Lamb's Supper* (New York: Doubleday, 1999), *Consuming the Word: The New Testament and the Eucharist in the Early Church* (New York: Image, 2013), and his forthcoming book on the mystery of faith (Steubenville, OH: Emmaus Road) all unpack the saving role of food for both ancient Israel and Christians.

There also are some books out there which pitch various forms of biblical diets and fasts. By now, though, you know my thoughts on such things.

CHAPTER 7: HOLY FAST—HUNGERING FOR CHRIST

If you really want to feel like a slacker in the ascetical life, read the Desert Fathers. In 2012, Oxford University Press put out an excellent one volume collection of their writings on fasting, holiness, and faith: *Philokalia: A Classic Text of Orthodox Spirituality.*

Caroline Walker Bynum's *Holy Feast, Holy Fast: The Religious Significance of Food to Medieval Woman* (Berkeley: University of

California Press, 1987) is the single best treatment of fasting I've come across. Her book *Fragmentation and Redemption: Essays on Gender and the Human Body in Medieval Religion* (New York: Zone Books, 1992) sheds further light on the topic.

Scott Hahn's *Signs of Life* (New York: Image, 2009) gives a good, basic primer on the tradition of fasting and the liturgical seasons. *The Origins of Feasts, Fasts, and Seasons in Early Christianity* (Collegeville, MN: Pueblo Books, 2011) by Paul Bradshaw and Maxwell Johnson goes even deeper.

CHAPTER 8: HOLY FEAST—REJOICING WITH CHRIST

For an excellent and engaging read on the Church's liturgical calendar and the feasts that populate it, read *The Feasts: How the Church Year Forms Us as Catholics* by Cardinal Donald Wuerl and Mike Aquilina (New York: Image, 2014).

For step-by-step guidance on how to celebrate those feasts, some of my favorite books include *The Handbook of Christian Feasts and Customs* by Fr. Francis X. Weiser (San Diego: Harcourt Brace & Company, 1952), *A Continual Feast* by Evelyn Birge Vitz (New York: Harper & Rowe, 1985), *The Catholic Home: Celebrations and Traditions for Holidays, Feast Days, and Every Day* by Meredith Gould (New York: Image, 2006), and *The Catholic Parent's Book of Feasts: Celebrating the Church Year with our Family* by Michaelann Martin, Carol Puccio, and Zoe Romanowsky (Huntington, IN: Our Sunday Visitor, 1999).

If you're looking for some saintly libations for your next feast, check out Michael Foley's fantastically fun *Drinking with the Saints: The Sinners Guide to a Holy Happy Hour* (Washington, DC: Regnery, 2015). Another fun cookbook mines the writings of Hildegard of

Bingen: *From Saint Hildegard's Kitchen: Foods of Health, Foods of Joy* (Liguori, MO: Liguori, 2010).

CHAPTER 9: TABLE LESSONS—EATING AND THE VIRTUES

My first introduction to the connection between eating and the virtues came in C. S. Lewis' *The Screwtape Letters* (San Francisco: Harper One, Reprint, 2015). Lewis putting his condemnation of gluttony into the words of a demon made that condemnation particularly effective for me. Dr. Edward Sri also did an excellent series of articles in *Lay Witness* on the virtues, including some which touched on eating. "Temperance and the Art of Eating," published in the May/June 2010 issue was particularly fine.

As for general primers on the virtues, good books abound. I would recommend starting with one of the following: *The Virtue Driven Life* by Fr. Benedict Groeschel (Huntington, IN: Our Sunday Visitor, 2006), *The Virtues* by Pope Benedict XVI (Huntington, IN: Our Sunday Visitor, 2010), or *Back to Virtue: Traditional Moral Wisdom for Modern Moral Confusion* by Peter Kreeft (San Francisco: Ignatius, 1992).

Donald DeMarco also did two wonderful books on the virtues: *The Heart of Virtue: Lessons from Life and Literature Illustrating the Beauty and Value of Moral Character* (San Francisco: Ignatius, 1996) and *The Many Faces of Virtue* (Steubenville, OH: Emmaus Road, 2000).

For the words of the masters on virtue, there's St. Thomas Aquinas' writings on the topic, collected in one volume, *On Virtues,* and translated by the English Dominican Province (CreateSpace, 2015) and St. Francis de Sales' *The Art of Loving* (Bedford, NH: Sophia Institute Press, 1998).

Lastly, although it has almost nothing to do with food, I also have to recommend Alasdair MacIntyre's assessment of contemporary culture and its lack of virtue, *After Virtue* (Notre Dame: IN: University of Notre Dame Press, 3rd Edition, 2007).

CHAPTER 10: SLAUGHTERING THE FATTED CALF—THE GIFT OF HOSPITALITY

I confess, I haven't read much on hospitality that I'm comfortable recommending. Most books I've come across on the topic confuse entertaining and hospitality and just reinforce an "entertaining as performance" mindset.

You can never go wrong reading about St. Benedict, though, who made hospitality part of the Benedictine Order's rule. The classic treatment of his life by Pope St. Gregory the Great is still in print, *The Life of Our Most Holy Father Saint Benedict* (London: Aeterna Press, 2015). There's also an interesting treatment of Benedictine hospitality called *Radical Hospitality: Benedict's Way of Love* by Fr. Daniel Hormon and Lonni Collins Pratt (Brewster, MA: Paraclete Press, 2011). It has some lovely insights on hospitality based on the lived experience of the monks. But it also has some fruity theology woven in, so you need to take some of the reflections with a grain of salt.

Even though it's not about hospitality directly, *The Little Oratory: A Beginners Guide to Praying in the Home* by Leila Lawler and David Clayton (Bedford, NH: Sophia Institute, 2014) offers some great thoughts about how to make your home a place where people want to be. Along similar lines, I'd also recommend Holly Pierot's *A Mother's Rule of Life: How to Bring Order to Your Home and Peace to Your Soul* (Bedford, NH: Sophia Institute, 2004), Hubert van Zeller's classic *Holiness for Housewives and Other Working*

Women (Bedford, NH: Sophia Institute, 1997), and Kimberly Hahn's *Graced and Gifted: Biblical Wisdom for the Homemaker's Heart* (Cincinnati: Servant Books, 2008).

CHAPTER 11: KITCHEN RULES—A PRACTICAL THEOLOGY OF FOOD

This one's all me. It's how I live the faith in my kitchen and at table. For more on the topic, visit my blog, www.thecatholictable.com.